THE BANNOCK BURN

The Joan Blaue Map of Scotland pictured above is reproduced with the kind permission of the National Library of Scotland.

Murray Cook & Ian McNeish

Other Books by
Murray Cook

Rituals, Roundhouses and Romans
[with Lindsay Dunbar]

Digging into Stirling's Past:
Uncovering the Secrets of Scotland's Smallest City

The Anvil of Scottish History: Stories of Stirling

Balbithan Wood, Kintore, Aberdeenshire:
The Evaluation of Prehistoric Landscapes

White Castle:
The Evaluation of an Upstanding Prehistoric Enclosure in East Lothian
[with David Connolly and Hana Kdolska]

Bannockburn and Stirling Bridge:
Exploring Scotland's Two Greatest Battles

Other Books by
Ian McNeish

The Fearn Bobby: Reflections from a Life in Scottish Policing

From Dumyat to Mont Blanc: Being Alive with Mountains

THE BANNOCK BURN

Journeys Along and Across the World's Most Famous Burn

Murray Cook & Ian McNeish

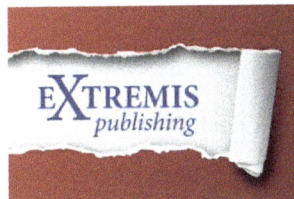

EXTREMIS
publishing

The Bannock Burn: Journeys Along and Across the World's Most Famous Burn by Murray Cook and Ian McNeish.

First edition published in Great Britain in 2022 by Extremis Publishing Ltd., Suite 218, Castle House, 1 Baker Street, Stirling, FK8 1AL, United Kingdom.

www.extremispublishing.com

Extremis Publishing is a Private Limited Company registered in Scotland (SC509983) whose Registered Office is Suite 218, Castle House, 1 Baker Street, Stirling, FK8 1AL, United Kingdom.

A CIP catalogue record for this book is available from the British Library.

ISBN: 978-1-7398543-3-1

Typeset in Sorts Mill Goudy, designed by The League of Moveable Type.

Printed and bound in Great Britain by IngramSpark, Chapter House, Pitfield, Kiln Farm, Milton Keynes, MK11 3LW, United Kingdom.

CONTENTS

This book is dedicated to
the wonderful people of historic
Stirlingshire and the Forth Valley.

THE BANNOCK BURN

Journeys Along and Across
the World's Most Famous Burn

Murray Cook & Ian McNeish

INTRODUCTION

If you've travelled north or south through Stirling, Scotland's smallest city,[1] you will have crossed a tiny wee sluggish burn—no more than 14.5 miles (23.3 km) long and 5m wide at high tide (blink and you will miss it). In fact, you would have just passed over the Bannock Burn,[2] which played a decisive role in the greatest battle of Scottish history and is named after it—or rather after the town that's named for the burn. But as you read on, you will discover that this slippery trickle of a stream has played an incredibly big role in Scottish history, twisting and turning, connecting events and people throughout our nation's story. This is because Stirling sits at the lowest crossing point of the River Forth, so if you went north or south you did it at Stirling and—to get to or from Stirling—you crossed the Bannock Burn. In fact, it took the construction of the Forth Rail Bridge in 1882—the biggest bridge in the world at the time—to finally bypass Stirling!

This means that everyone in Scottish history from the Romans to the Jacobites, from Queen Victoria to William Wallace and Bonnie Prince Charlie, that every invader trying to steal our wee bit hill and glen, that every hero who bled for our freedom has crossed the Bannock Burn. Again and again, the Bannock Burn flows and intertwines through Scottish history and, if this is not enough, it is also connected to the colonisation of Nova Scotia, cuts through a fossilised sea to run into a lost one, involves Moss Lairds, Celtic brochs and hillforts, and lies at the heart of the creation of tartan.

Of the two authors, Murray is Stirling Council's archaeologist whose job it is to protect, explore and share the city's rich history, all of which is crammed into a tiny place. He has walked most of the burn over the years, sometimes for work and sometime for fun, but every trip revealing something new. Thinking that this might be a good story, he approached his pal Ian McNeish and they decided to walk the burn together and then to write this book. This of course means that the tone of the book changes as to which of us is writing—we hope that this is charming rather than irritating.

Ian says he is a 'bulge baby', born in 1946 directly after World War II and brought up in small industrial towns across central Scotland as his parents moved about following employment opportunities. He had a few jobs when leaving school, from working in an iron foundry to building electronic parts for the Kestrel Jump jet and the legendary Concorde aircraft. He then headed to Harlow in Essex when he was nineteen years of age and worked for an electronics company. After four years there he headed north to Aberdeen, working for the County Council. At the age of twenty-seven he headed even further north and joined Ross and Sutherland constabulary. Five years later he was moved to a force in the centre of Scotland. On retiring in 2004, he teamed up with an ex-colleague and set up in business: a venture that led him to becoming the Chairman of the Board of a community-based drug and alcohol charity. Ian finally retired—well nearly—in 2016.

Ian had, and still leads, an active life. This included football, then rugby, before heading into the mountains—an activity that saw him climb all the Munros as well as Mont Blanc, and serving in a mountain rescue team. He is a keen photographer and plays curling, and won the Scottish Police Curling Championship twice. He is also an enthusiastic cyclist. When not doing any of the above, he reads and writes. He is married, has three sons and six grandchildren.

In terms of writing, Ian has always maintained an interest in writing, and for a while maintained two blogs. It was the latter activity that opened a door into the writing world he is now privileged to occupy. Nearly four years ago the owner of Extremis Publishing, an independent publisher based in Stirling—where he now lives—contacted him and asked him to write two books. The first of these, *The Fearn Bobby*, published in 2018, is a very personal account of his experiences as a police officer. Ian's second book, *From Dumyat to Mont Blanc: Being Alive with Moun-*

tains, launched in 2020 and is a meandering tale of his life-changing mountain experiences, motivations and more.

This book tells the story of our trips down and across the burn, and how you might follow in our footsteps. We will reveal the best of the stories we discovered and let you know why we think the Bannock Burn is the most famous burn in the world.

While the burn itself measures only 14.5 miles, if you walk the route we describe you will walk roughly 19 miles (30 km), as there is a bit of doubling back on yourself back at the start and end. While there are large sections with track, most of the route is without it—you will be walking over rough ground, crossing fences and the burn itself several times, so you will need good waterproof boots or wellies.

Though it is possible to do the walk in a long day, we decided to do it in four stages, between useful parking spots. The book is broken into those four sections, each with its own map showing the route we took. Each

Near the start... a wee trickle of a thing!

starts with a place to park and describes where to cross the fence and the river and details any alternative routes, followed by how we did it and what we discovered as our host, the Bannock Burn, took us for a walk. It's important to stress that the maps mark our recommended route and not the one we took, which is harder and in some places far more dangerous. Ultimately the choice is yours.

What's in a Name?

Just like Scotland today, Bannockburn is a hybrid. It contains both Gaelic (Bannock) and Scots (burn, meaning stream), reflecting that

Scots was already replacing Gaelic as Scotland's language in the 14th century. But what does it mean? As this is Scotland, there are several versions and at least one tall tale. Let's start with the myth: 'bannock' is also a type of bread in Scotland and there is, according to tradition, a prophecy by the 14th century seer Sir Thomas de Ercildoun (also known as Thomas the Rhymer): '*The burn of breid, sall run fow reid*' ('*the burn of bread shall run full red*'). It is not clear if this couplet was indeed one of Thomas' or rather a later composition ascribed to him. Certainly when asked, in around 1310, by the countess of Dunbar when the war would end,[3] he replied that it would end when the 'Bannockburn is donged with dead men' (full of bodies). Oh, very chilling; but it's worth noting that while he was a real person there are no contemporary accounts of him accurately prophesying anything, so—like so many Scots heroes—his reputation likely grew in the telling.

Another option is that 'bannock' is a corruption of the Gaelic *ban oc*, meaning 'the white, shining stream'. This would mean that the Bannockburn literally means *the white, shining stream stream*. This semantic overlap is a fairly common process when one language comes to dominate another, and still happens today. You may have visited Inchcolm, an island in the Forth, whose name is Scots and Gaelic for 'St Columba's Isle'—Columba shortened to Colm, and Inch meaning island in Gaelic. To add a third language to the mix, as we now speak English rather than Scots, you will increasingly find the place being described as the Isle of Inchcolm!

The third option is both the coolest and most agreed upon as the best, and doesn't really contradict the second. The first poem written in and about what became Scotland is *The Goddodin*, one of a series of tales from the *Hengerdd* (the Old North). The Old North is the broader term which describes the region encompassing the north of England and southern Scotland, an area which fell to the invading pagan Angles to become the Kingdom of Northumbria. The loss and destruction of Christian British Kingdoms in the face of invading pagan Angles and Saxons, is of course the core background to the Arthurian myth cycle. A brief flash of heroic resistance, where the tide is stopped before rising again and overwhelming the last dying light in the west.[4] Indeed, *The Goddodin* contains the oldest mention of King Arthur. Now, many people thinking of this and Stirling and Falkirk get very excited about Camelon (a small town outside Falkirk) and the similarity of the word to the legendary Camelot. The core of Camelon is a 1st century Roman fort, and this has led to even more speculation—might King Arthur be from Falkirk? However, Camelot doesn't appear in the older Arthurian stories; it's a later addition. But that doesn't mean that the context is wrong; people here fought the invading Angles, and viewed Arthur as a hero.

Anyway, to return to *The Goddodin*, which survives only in archaic Welsh and which describes 300 heroes assembling in a great lord's hall in around AD 600, being fed, entertained and getting very drunk before heading off into a glorious battle where they are defeated in a suitably heroic manner (a bit like following Scotland in the World Cup!). The poem includes elegies for many of the fallen and one of the heroes is Llif, son of Cian. He is described as being from beyond Bannawc, a location thought to be the hills between Cambusbarron and Fintry, and this of course is where the Bannock Burn rises. So Bannock Burn might be 'the Burn from Bannawc'. But what does Bannawc mean? It's possible that the Ban- bit is a corruption of *ben*- which means mountain in Gaelic, making Bannock Burn literally 'the burn from the hills'.[5]

However, let's return to our fallen hero Llif, whose elegy (which is quite stilted[6]) is as follows:

When he repaired to his native country, his fame was spread abroad;
He poured out the wine, the golden-torqued man!
He would give a gorgeously fine suit to a brave person,
And check a hundred men, courteous hero!
And send away the progeny of a foreign knight;
The only son of Cian from beyond Bannawc,
Never did in Goddodin tread on the surface of the fosse,
While he was, any one more ardent than Lliv.

St Ninians Parish

Now, the entire length of our Bannock Burn runs through the Parish of St Ninians. In Scotland, parishes are the ancient boundaries which determined how the church was organised, and they are all different sizes. That difference has always interested people; in theory, parishes are like Parliamentary Constituencies and should contain roughly the same number of people each. This means that in poorer land parishes are bigger than in richer land, as the capacity of the land is greater. Now many people—including my late friend Alasdair Ross—have argued that perhaps the parish system may be pre-Christian and appears to relate to civil organisation. Sometimes parishes have isolated separate patches, which contain a type of resource not present in the main one. All of this is very exciting, and lets us get a glimpse into the roots of Scotland.

St Ninians Kirk... was he really here?

But who was St Ninian? Traditionally he converted the people of southern Scotland to Christianity, but it's not entirely clear that this really happened. Certainly southern Scotland was converted, but it took more than one person. One of the earliest dedications to St Ninian, and one that is attached to an ancient church foundation, is St Ninians church—from which the parish takes its name. The church was originally called Eggles, from Gaelic for *ecclesia*. However, the origins of the conversion are shrouded in mystery, if for no other reason than that the first Christians in Britain—when it was part of the Roman Empire—had to practise in secret as it was against the law. It's likely that St Ninian was retroactively given a much bigger role to help explain a process later generations struggled to understand. Now, if you think that the early church was incapable of being slippery with the truth, do you really think St Andrew's remains were carried from Greece to Fife? Although, perhaps he really liked golf? Saying that, it does seem entirely possible that the real St Ninian was actually present in Stirling, as our dedication appears to be one of the earliest.

Now, when we were writing this book our conversations slid into just about everything. Ian's brother now lives in Texas, so we obviously got talking about Texas and the Alamo one day and Ian said they were all Scots (Sam Houston, Davy Crockett and Jim Bowie).[7] Being a fan of all things tenuously Scottish, Murray added that they would have descended from Scottish migrants from the 17th or 18th centuries. Murray of course also brought up Elvis Presley and John Wayne,[8] both of whose origins lie in our bonnie country! Something flashed in Ian's eyes and he asked if the Bowies were not from Stirling? Murray didn't know, so Ian phoned the good people at The Alamo. Now opinions vary as to exactly what happened at the Alamo and who were the villains of the piece, but we're sticking to the official version, which begins with the universal, unending struggle between or against the status quo for independence and self-determination. In that way, the Texas Revolution has parallels with our local battle, fought on the banks of our host, the Bannock Burn, in 1314. One combatant in the more recent battle arguably strengthens that connection.

During the years 1835–36 the northern Mexican region Coahuilla y Texas became embroiled in revolution. On one side was Mexico and on the other a mixture of local Mexican residents (Tejanos), supported by settlers from further north. To this day that bloody conflict is known as the Texas Revolution.

Mexico lost its hold on the area and, in March 1836, the new breakaway realm declared its independence. Thus was born the Republic of Texas. Texas was admitted to the Union in December 1845, becoming the 28th State in the Union of the United States of America.

Perhaps the most pivotal and famous battle of that revolution was The Alamo, or to be more correct: the Mission San Antonia de Valero. A Mission that was set up by Franciscan missionaries in 1718, founded as a base to convert the Pampoa, Suliajame, and Pastia peoples to Christianity. It was abandoned towards the end of that century, during the Mexican struggle to be independent from Spain. A few decades later, during the Texas Revolution, it was occupied again, this time by a group of about 180 of the 'revolutionaries', mostly Texans and Tejanos. The Mexican army, four thousand strong, led by President General Antonio López de Santa Anna, laid siege to the Alamo and for thirteen days the inhabitants stubbornly resisted against overwhelming odds before being overrun, with the majority being killed. Santa Anna then reclaimed the city of San Antonio for Mexico.

Because of the bravery shown by the inhabitants against those odds—and perhaps how it was depicted by Hollywood—one would almost think it had been a victory.[9] Amongst those who fought and died were some of the most iconic names in the history of Texas and the USA: William Travis, Davy Crockett and our own local connection, Colonel James Bowie (famous for the Bowie knife). The museum staff at The Alamo claim his family hailed from our parish of St Ninians.

Now, exactly who were these Bannockburn Bowies, and was there any truth in the claim? According to an 1899 book (*The Bowies and Their Kindred*) by one Walter Worthington Bowie, there is some credence to the idea—as we shall see. There is little doubt that the Bowie name has been prevalent in the Stirling area for centuries, and it seems likely that Bowie is a phonetic spelling of the Gaelic *buidhe* (pronounced, 'booaie' or 'booay'), which appears to mean 'golden'—in some contexts it may refer to grateful, agreeable or perhaps lucky. It can be traced to some place names, for example

Jim Bowie monument in New Boston, Bowie County. Photo by Paul Ridenour.

Killbuie and Loch Buie on Mull. Not forgetting Auchenbowie, hardly a skimming stone away from the Bannock Burn. The ancient family crest of Bowie, or Buidhe, bore '*argent on a bend sable and three buckles*,' similar to the Stirlings'—which perhaps hints at an ancient link. Certainly, the Church of the Holy Rude, Stirling's main medieval church, once had a chapel called 'Bowye's Iyle.'

Later Bowies appear through the church records of both Stirling and Falkirk, for example the parish register of Stirling mentions a John Bowye in 1553 and a few years later a James and a William Bowie. The Burgess of Falkirk 1623 was a John Bowie and in 1737 there was another William Bowie, magistrate of Stirling. It is these Bowies that Walter links to the Texan one in a general, roundabout way, but are you convinced? Well, regardless, we think you will agree, the connections are strong and the possibility of such a link should not be discarded willy-nilly. And anyway, why, of all the place names in Scotland that could have been cited, did those responsible for the modern Alamo, pick St Ninians as the place Jim Bowie's ancestors hailed from?

The Scottish Outdoor Access Code
American friends are always amazed when we stop a car and climb a fence in some random location to show them something. They're always wondering if they'll get into trouble or shot! But I always proudly exclaim that this is Scotland (think '*This is Sparta!*') and we have the right to roam where we wish. But with rights come responsibilities, and you must respect the countryside and those whose livelihoods depend on it and follow the Scottish Outdoor Access Code.

In short: leave gates as you find them, don't walk through people's gardens or fields of crops, avoid walking through the middle of stock, don't make loud noises, climb gates at the hinges and use strainers, keep dogs on leashes and always take your litter away with you. And most importantly of all, don't do anything you'd be ashamed to tell your granny about.

Also it's worth noting that certain sections of the route have no mobile phone reception, that large chunks have no formal or informal paths, and that you should always wear appropriate clothes. Please let people know where you have gone and take care crossing the roads. Finally, at each key point we have included both the National Grid Reference and the Longitude and Latitude, the Grid reference uses the numeric scale and not the alphanumeric system.

* * *

Endnotes

1) See Murray's book *Digging into Stirling's Past* for more details about this wonderful place!

2) So while the town and the battle are Bannockburn the stream is the Bannock Burn, though you will find the off use of Bannockburn to mean the stream.

3) It ran from 1296 to 1328, though the Battle of Bannockburn in 1314 was the key turning point.

4) Tolkien readers will also find this echoed in the migration of the elves as they leave Middle-earth for the West.

5) It's worth noting another Bannockburn in Sutherland, near the town of Helmsdale. It's about 13km long and originates on a hill called Knockfin near the village of Kinbrace, before merging with its larger neighbour, the River Helmsdale. Two rivers, situated at opposite ends of the country, with no obvious historical connection sharing the same name, and both flow out of hilly areas. I think the case is won!

6) A better, more poetic translation is from Professor Thomas Owen Clancy and is available in his book *The Triumph Tree*.

7) While these chaps were of course second to third generation Scots, there were a few more recent immigrants at the Alamo including one that played the bagpipes to keep everyone's spirits up.

8) Hmm. We can hear the scepticism, but John Wayne's father, a Morrison, was from Caithness and there is still a Presley's butcher in Old Meldrum.

9) The British Empire was also very good at this sort of thing: think of Tennyson's poem 'The Charge of The Light Brigade' or General Gordon's suicidal mission in Khartoum.

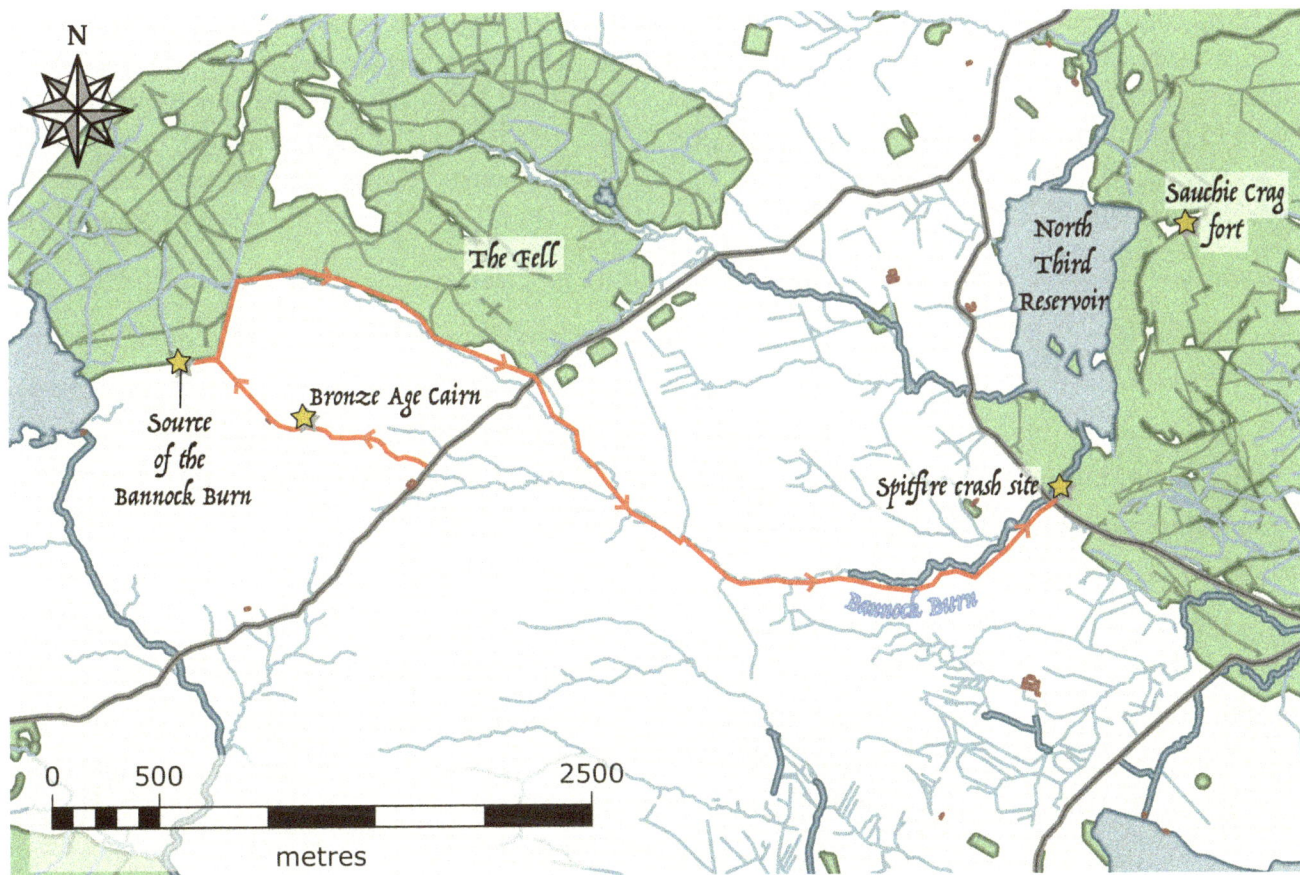

N

The Fell

Source
of the
Bannock Burn

Bronze Age Cairn

North
Third
Reservoir

Sauchie Crag
fort

Spitfire crash site

Bannock Burn

0   500   2500

metres

The Direct Route: 4.4 miles (7.06 km)

The start of the route is the bellmouth at the bottom of Earl's Hill (*272590, 688191, 56° 04' 10" N 4° 02' 54" W*), where there is no parking, though there is some a 10 minute walk away to the north (*273128, 688638, 56° 04' 25" N 4° 02' 23" W*). Take the rough metalled track to the communication masts at the top of the hill. At the summit head north-west to the corner of the conifer woodland below you (*271591, 688738, 56° 04' 27" N 4° 03' 52" W*). The ground here is heather which while bonny can trip you up, so take care. Cross into the forest and walk down to the source of the Bannock Burn (*271420, 688737, 56° 04' 27" N 4° 04' 02" W*) watch out though as the ground is very rough with lots of hidden drains. From the source of the burn you can either follow it through the wood or walk back up the hill and around the outside of the wood, before catching the burn again in the clear. Follow the burn back down to the road (*273073, 688571, 56° 04' 23" N 4° 02' 26" W*), there are a handful of sheep tracks on the northern bank of the burn but no proper track. Cross the road and just to your left is a gate into the next field. Again follow the burn, every now and again there will be sheep tracks and lines from quad bikes and there are a few fences to cross. Eventually, you will hit a rough track for shooting parties (*273823, 687859, 56° 04' 01" N 4° 01' 42" W*) which you can take or you can continue following the burn. You will eventually hit the road at next at North Third (*275602, 688040, 56° 04' 08" N 3° 59' 59" W*) and there are several areas of informal parking.

How We Did It

The Bannock Burn rises below the rounded summit of Earl's Hill (441m od), the second highest peak in the Campsies; there are tremendous views in all directions. To the south-west of the summit is Earl's Burn and the Carron Valley, to the east Falkirk, and to the west the peak of Ben Lomond. Earl's Hill itself bristles with telecommunications masts, and there are clusters of wind turbines and industry in almost every direction. While to the north-east is Stirling—the 'cradle of kings, who set their castle strong on its high ridge', as medieval poet Arthur Johnston described it—and beyond the looming Ochils.

Murray's first time up the hill was just before dawn in a frosty November, with a full fat hunter's moon and the warning whirring and drumming of the grouse as they sped off, unseen round his periphery. Though when both of us did it was cold, wet and very windy,

The source of the Bannock Burn.

Murray on the Earl's Hill burial cairn at dawn, with Ben Lomond in the distance.

with Ian nursing a slowly worsening limp, Murray's feet beginning to squelch, and his wife's plaintive suggestion to perhaps reschedule it to another day ringing in our ears (as Burns would have it, 'the sage advices the husband from the wife despises!') and we nearly gave the whole thing up... but you must always at least expect a little bad weather in Scotland!

A Long Forgotten Grave
The hill and its environs are dominated by intrusive modernity, communication pylons and wind turbines, which of course is why there's an easy track all the way to the summit.

All of them dwarf a possible prehistoric burial cairn (271838, 688435, 56° 04′ 17″ N 4° 03′ 38″ W), located right at the summit and a little battered by their construction. Burial cairns are deliberate piles of stones that were built to both bury the dead and to secure rights to the land (the climate was warmer at the time!). The more you bury your ancestors in the land, the easier it is to say it's always been yours. Can you picture mourners gathered round the cairn, stifling tears and remembering their loved one? In the distance to the west is the magnificent Ben Lomond, perhaps at the time revered as a god or goddess.

Earl's Hill and Earl's Burn are often linked to either the Earldoms of Lennox or Stirling. Certainly, the hill stands at the border between them. However, the Earldom of Stirling was created in 1633 and Earl's Burn appears on maps from the 1500s, so it's more likely that the burn represents the ancient boundary of the Earldom of Lennox. This perhaps means that the hill was named for the burn. However, it first appears in the late 17th century, so perhaps it was named after the Stirling Earldom?

The Earldom of Lennox was founded in the 12th century, and the first Earl was the future David I. The Lennox, or the *Lemhnaig* in Gaelic, originally appears to have been separate from Scotland (or Alba[10] as it was known), as it is listed in the early 11th century along with Alba as giving tribute to the King of Munster, Brian Boruma. David I was also known as the Prince of the Cumbrians (which meant Strathclyde at the time) and both these titles seem to reflect the expansion of the early Scottish kingdom from its core, swallowing whole smaller independent kingdoms. Stirling of course sat between Strathclyde, the Lennox and Alba, and let's not forget the Angles to the south-east—strategically very important, but battered and bruised through years of conflict between all these warring groups. Where we stood probably represented a no man's land frontier zone, lawless and cold and empty (some things never change).

Returning to the Earl of Stirling, the first Earl, William Alexander, was appointed by Charles I, who famously believed in the divine right of kings and tried to tell parliament what to do—and all that power went to his head, and he lost it. William was the son of the fifth Earl of Menstrie and his

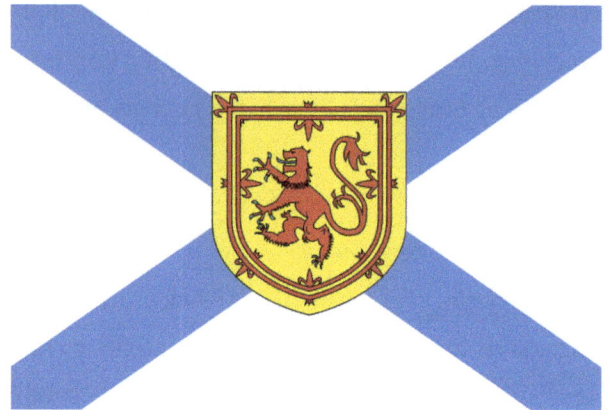

The Nova Scotian Flag.

4

ancestral seat is the eponymous castle. He appears to have sponsored the first precious metal extraction from the Ochils. Earlier in his life, before he was an Earl, William had founded Nova Scotia in 1621, which was apparently to be based on James VI's Plantation of Ulster (an incredibly bad idea, with effects still being felt nearly 400 years later!). Eventually William became Viscount of Canada, but lost most of his money and Nova Scotia was returned to the French in 1632. However, William's coat of arms still features on the Nova Scotian flag. He was also a prolific poet and, dear reader, Murray has read some of his verse in research for this book. Be grateful we have decided not to quote it, as it is rather dated and dull; a poor man's Donne in our humble opinion! Anyway, William died in London in 1640 at the age of 60, and was buried in the Church of

Snapping jaws of death...
the gin trap.

the Holy Rude in the now-vanished Earl of Stirling's Aisle (the one that had been called the Bowie Lyle). Unfortunately, having lost the aisle, the title also vanished in 1739 with the death of the fifth Earl. As for the Earl of Lennox, the first run of that title vanished when its bearer, Murdoch Duke of Albany, plotted against his nephew, James I, who responded by executing his uncle and two of his cousins on the Beheading Stone on Mote Hill in 1425—although the next generation in turn assassinated James I, who died in a drain under a tennis court in Perth. Now that's what you call a family feud!

Moving north-west from the peak, we walked and stumbled over dense heather towards the corner of the commercial conifer plantation, where there's an old rusty gate with a broken

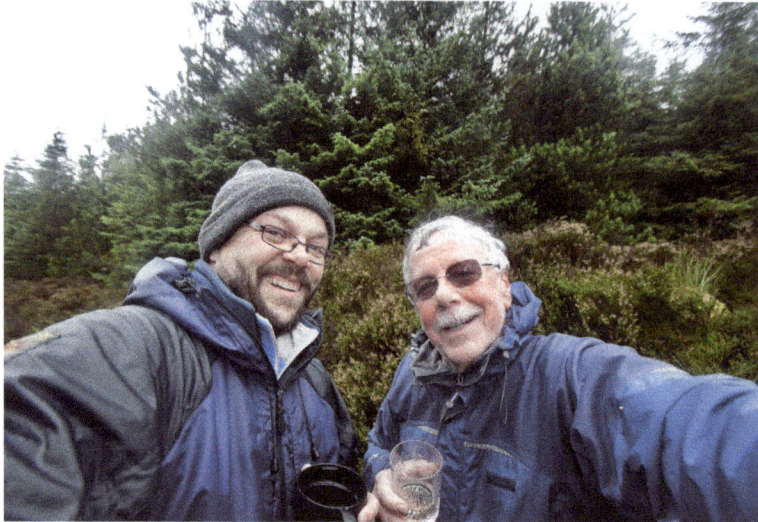

Straight from the source...a refreshing drink from the Bannock Burn.

bounding off no guide. The first time Murray went up, he got lost twice—whose idea was this, anyway?

We took the far easier way and followed the fence back up the hill and around the wood, turned left at the corner with the strainer cemented into a glacial erratic, and back down into the burn valley. Beyond the woods, the burn emerges and begins to carve a valley, bubbling and jumping across the side of Earl's Hill. It becomes easier to follow but the way is still rough going, and full of holes and hidden cracks. Murray fell up to his waist three times, his wellies squelching all the way back to the road. Ian's foot began to cramp, and Murray apologised for the ground being much rougher than promised. Needless to say, the ground did not care!

The heather beneath our feet writhed with darting voles. There's no path here; just the odd sheep track, though the ground is easier on the north side of the burn. To the south, this portion is an active grouse moor and you'll see the grouse butts as you walk down,

gin trap on it. Gin traps and their cruel snapping jaws are now illegal, but were a barbaric way to catch rabbits and foxes.

The source of the burn rises in a small area of damp boggy moss and to your right in a gap in the trees. All you detect at first is the water's gurgle until a brown peaty trickle bursts out from the peat—lovely and refreshing; bring a cup! But blink and the burn is gone, becoming a boggy morass curving between the dense pines. There's no path, it's hard going and very disorientating, the white flashes of deer so—whatever you do—please make sure you don't get shot during the season!

Eventfully you hit the road, an unnamed single lane that will take you to Fintry if you turn right or to Stirling if you turn left, not that you would know—you could be anywhere in Scotland. But our journey is straight over and through the gate, where the ground levels out. There is still no track, and you will have to cross the burn a few times as well as climb the odd fence, the barbed wire of which ripped Murray's waterproof trousers (and they were new, too!).

The start of Swallowhaugh and the first bing of quarry waste, with Earl's Hill in the background.

Quarrying a Lost Ocean
About two kilometers south east of the point where the Bannock Burn seeps and percolates into the light of day through a bright green patch of sphagnum moss, you will encounter the first glen-like feature in the initially gently sloping, hummock strewn, ankle bending, peat bog journey of our host (274027, 687743, 56° 03′ 57″ N 4° 01′ 30″ W).

While we refer to it as a glen, that seems too grand a word, so perhaps we should use ripple. Its formal name is Swallowhaugh which appears on some 18th century references; a name that has disappeared from current maps, more's the pity. Haugh, from old Scots *hawgh* or *hauch*, literally means 'defile'—an archaic word for a narrow pass through hills. The older name has something rustic and mystical about it, and is certainly more descriptive than present day offerings. Whatever name one will confer, there is something that is certain: it is more like a shallow fold in the landscape than any grand sweeping highland glen, and does not become visually obvious until you are almost upon it. Though in summer, the arcs and loups of the swallows tend to give it away.

Once in Swallowhaugh, the Bannock Burn drops step by step in height as it tumbles and gurgles over a few flat sill edges, more pleasing on the eye and ear than threatening. However, it is not the visual grandeur, or lack thereof, one encounters when transiting through this narrow pass that raises its status and your interest. Unsuspectingly, you have been lured into an ancient world of oceans, moving continents, fossils and industrial innovation.

So, where are we? There was a time, well in excess of 500 million years ago, when the place you are walking through, and much of the land we now call Scotland (certainly the far north and far west) originated in a continent called Laurentia. The remainder of the land, along with England, was on a separate continent called Gondwana. Both were located south of the equator, separate neighbours in the Lapetus Ocean. Present day England and a large part of Scotland were totally separate then, and only joined together at the end of a series of geological events known as the Caledonian Orogeny, around 450 million years ago. But that is another story. Mind you, had it not happened, would Scotland have been born and would the battle named after our burn ever have taken place?

During these far off times, rainforests, warm seas and rivers covered large parts of what we

A long dead crinoid fossil from way before the Bannock Burn.

now call Central Scotland. The seas and rivers abounded with coral reefs, flora and fauna, including crabs and other crustaceans. The decay and accumulation of the forests over millennia produced layers of coal, while the crushed corals, bivalves, brachiopods and crinoids produced limestone. For the next mile or so, the walk takes us over this long dead sea and the Bannock Burn exposes layers of limestone which formed the basis of a medieval industry with world-wide links! Also, from this point all the way to the next stage at North Third there is a well-used track and gates through the two fences.

So what is so significant about sedimentary rock embedded with fossilised sea creatures? The answer is Calcium Oxide, contained in the fossil remains. Limestone-rich soils are more fertile and, as we shall see, formed the basis of a uniquely dense cluster of Celtic fortifications. However, if the limestone could be quarried it could be transported and used elsewhere, and there are records of lime from this area being used from the 16th century while the first mapped quarries date to the mid-18th century. But this is a tricky process;

it has to be quarried and then broken up and calcined, ('burned' at above 840°C), which causes the fossils contained therein to decompose into calcium oxide, better known as burnt lime, quicklime or simply lime. Calcium oxide has various useful qualities, particularly in the production of mortar and plaster for building and in the manufacture of iron. It is a source of calcium and magnesium for plants, increasing the pH of acidic soils, and in doing so increasing yield (it is not unknown for eggshells and oyster shells to have been used for the same purpose). It could also be used in bleaching, medicines, tanning, sugar production and the disposal of corpses and more.

It is no surprise therefore that lime extraction has played an important role in societies for centuries. Evidence of primitive lime kilns are to be found all over Scotland, and far and wide across the globe. Allow your imagination to take you back, not just three hundred years and not just within the boundaries of Scotland, but further back in time and well beyond our borders. We can find some of the earliest references to lime in the Old Testament, e.g. Isaiah 33:12: 'And people shall be as the burning of lime, as thorns cut down, that are burned in the fire.'

Let us return to our Bannock Burn. As you progress, you will pass a number of grass covered mounds along the banks of your host for the day. On closer inspection, you will see that several are small pyramid-shaped mounds, while others are horseshoe or 'U' shaped. You have just encountered the first evidence of the burn's industrial past: 18th century lime workings. These stretch for about a kilometre along the Bannock Burn at this point, where it is flanked on its south side by Drummarnock Hill.

A warning to the curious when in this area: be on the lookout for a ghost—not the last to be encountered on this journey. On the far side of the hill you are passing, Drummarnock Hill, is a mound, thought by antiquarians to be a place of Druidical Sepulture: the grave of a druid.[11] It certainly was the scene of a burial, as a stone cist and a skeleton were discovered

A clamp kiln and its landscape.

in the mound, interestingly called, to this day: Ghost's Knowe. The axe, found at the time the grave was opened, was later removed, so will not be in the possession of the ghost. One less thing to worry about!

Back to the lime workings. The commonest of these early lime kilns, certainly in Scotland, are known as clump or clamp kilns—also known in some areas as common or sow kilns and further afield, heap kilns. Whatever name one chooses, these early kilns were quite simple affairs. The first job in the process of lime extraction was to access a nearby source of limestone and transport it to the kilns. The north flank of Drummarnock Hill is scarred with broken and exposed rock faces.

These were where the raw limestone rock was quarried out of the hillside to be burned in the clamps.[12] That was, certainly in the 18th and 19th centuries, typically carried out by the use of crowbars and large hammers. On occasion, it may well have been blasted with gunpowder.

A quarried landscape.

The first quarries were simply clawed and carved from the side of the valley, where the burn had exposed the geology, but gradually the quarries got bigger and there is also a series of cold, damp mines running underground. As we will see below, some are still open, though please don't explore them.

The rock was smashed into smaller pieces to aid the process. The shattered limestone and the fuel (peat, timber, brushwood and in some cases coal), would then be built up in alternate layers and covered with stone or turf to form a mound. Holes were left in the mound to aid ventilation and keep the fire going, which took hours. After leaving time for cooling, the mound would be burst open to access the burnt lime.

These early kilns were not very efficient and the random layering of limestone and combustibles often led to uneven heat distribution, with some rocks being under-heated and others being overheated, the former being unconverted and the latter fused. Because of this, the volume of burnt lime produced was inconsistent, and resulted in the products having to be sorted and sieved by hand. It was dirty work, covering the workers in lime dust which could produce an intense chemical burn.[13] The kiln, if carefully opened and emptied, could be rebuilt and used again. The majority of the visible workings you will encounter as you pass along this part of the Bannock Burn, are what remains of these early, primitive 'clamp kilns' and spoil heaps.

We spent a lot of time wandering round looking at them and keeping our eyes peeled

The fiery red heat of a 400 year old lime kiln under excavation.

for fossils of the little creatures who died all those millions of years ago. There are at least 46 surviving kilns, but it's likely that far more have been destroyed or buried by later quarrying or farming. There is also a series of great views of the valley and the exposed geology, but of course this means you have to cross and recross the burn. Which is fine if you're sprightly and flexible, but Ian can get a bit stiff so we lost half an hour as he had to trek back—so you've been warned!

In 2017, Murray helped set up a small project with the late Professor Paul Bishop of Glasgow University to use archaeomagnetic dating to try to date two of these small clamp kilns. This uses changes in the earth's magnetic signal to calculate when stone or pottery was last melted and indicated that the kilns were used in the 17th century, the same time as the 1st Earl of Stirling.

Initially, lime was quarried for use as mortar, to both bind stones and as render on building exteriors. It seems possible that some of the Bannock Burn lime was used on the Great Hall, the slightly lurid building at the heart of

Stirling and its Great Hall... the largest in Scotland.

boggy carse around Stirling to the fertile farmland we know today, famed for the production of Timothy Hay which is a key source in race horse diets. We will return to the clearing of the bog later on but this period, known as the Improvements (which led to the Highland Clearances), resulted in a 300% increase in economic output!

Stirling Castle. This was built by King James IV, when Stirling was his proud, independent capital. Completed in 1503, it remains the largest Great Hall ever built in Scotland. The colour, Royal Gold, is the actual colour picked by James and was meant to be vivid and eye catching. Famously, the Great Hall was the scene of the magnificent feast for the baptism of James VI's son in 1594, in which the fish course was served in an enormous wooden ship complete with firing guns![14]

From the 17th century and increasingly across the 18th, lime was used as fertiliser, and this lay behind the conversion of the low-lying

As demand for lime increased, so it became obvious that these small clamp kilns could not supply the demand, and as we shall see the workings moved nearer Stirling and got much bigger, even becoming mines. Meanwhile, the kilns got larger and ever more efficient, and ended up looking almost like castles. These are called draw or periodic kilns; some are even Scheduled Monuments.

A Refreshing Break!
Now Murray is still young enough to enjoy a dook, and for the non-Scots, a dook is not quite a swim but so much more than a paddle—a bit like an ice-cold shock and then

Are you brave enough for a dook in The Bannock Burn?

if the sheep gaze on, horrified that anyone could be so stupid.

An Ancient Battle Axe

As you descend to lower ground and take your leave of the ancient lime workings, following in the ghostly hoof prints of heavily-laden work ponies from two centuries before, just at the point your gradual descent ends and you encounter a flat section of your walk, with the cliffs of Lewis Hill still a few hundred yard in front, look closely to your left and you will see a small stream intruding into our Bannock Burn from the west. Two hundred yards or so west of that confluence, along the invading stream, is a farm called Todholes. Near that dwelling, sometime in the 1920s, another piece of the ancient history that adorns this wonderful burn you are following was found: a 'Lava Battle-axe'. The axe was found by George MacDonald from Cambusbarron. As the name suggests, the axe was fashioned from volcanic rock, in this case mainly basalt with porphyritic feldspar crystals. It was probably made from stone located in the nearby Touch

out again. The limestone plates and their geology have a created a series of stunning waterfalls and wee plunge pools all along this section of the burn which are irresistible on a warm summer's day; indeed, he has been known to dook in his pants (which is not a euphemism for anything!). Swimming in Scotland is not for the faint-hearted; the water is very cold, and the bases of these pools are very uneven so watch your ankles. However, there is nothing as refreshing or bracing, even

Hills, which are ancient lava flows.

Such axes tend to be small with a central circular hole (for hafting). Our Bannock Burn axe, which dates to the Early to Middle Bronze Age (in the region of 1800 to 1600 BC), measures 14cm long and about 8cm at its widest. When first fashioned, it would have been an attractive speckled stone with a smooth finish. Despite their warlike name, there is little evidence they were weapons and instead likely fulfilled a range of functions, including use as tools, woodworking, land clearance, animal slaughter, and some perhaps as 'ceremonial objects'. They were often deposited in burials but also occur as single finds.

There have been finds of similar axes throughout Europe and, to date, thirty of these ancient, concave-sided, perforated axes,

The lava battle axe. Image kindly provided by William Gillies.

have been unearthed in Scotland, with the most (two!) from Stirling. The other Stirling axe was found in 1885 at the east end of what is now Torbrex, near where the old ice rink was and very near to the new High School of Stirling.[15] It is estimated to be from the same era as our Bannock Burn Axe, and is kept at The National Museum of Scotland.

This section of our walk ends at a modern concrete bridge over what was once a ford over the Bannock Burn. This is a very popular spot, and there is lots of informal parking.

* * *

Endnotes

10) Which at the time only extended from the Spey to the Forth.

11) Have you noticed it's always a druid with these antiquarians; was no one else ever buried?

12) Our source on the lime industry is an article in volume 2 of the *Forth Natural Historian*, by K.J.H. Mackay, entitled: 'Limestone Working: A Forgotten Stirlingshire Industry'.

13) The ancient Chinese used to punish offenders by applying lime to their eyes.

14) Sounds a bit like a Borgia family birthday bash.

15) Which is nearly 900 years old itself, so has moved around a bit.

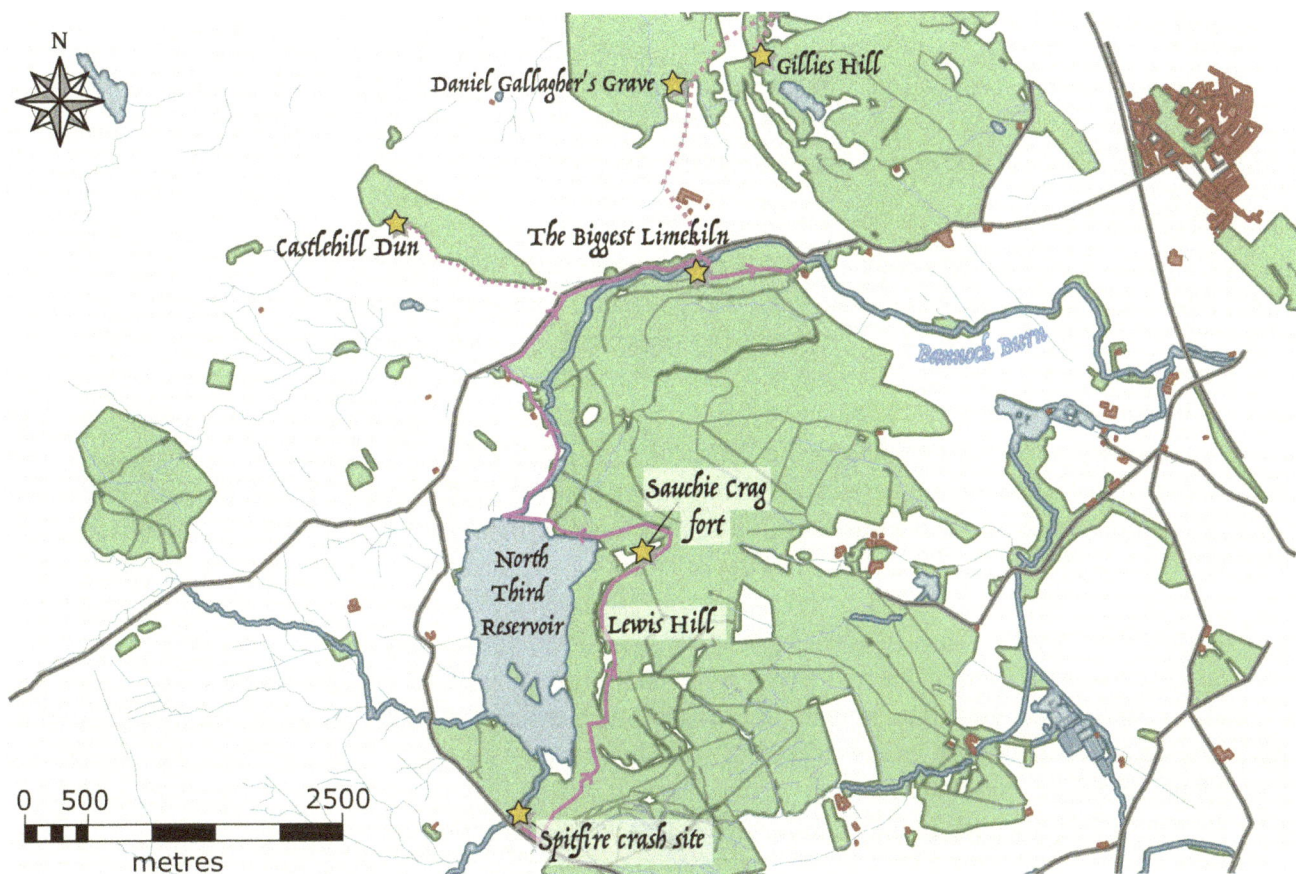

N

Daniel Gallagher's Grave

Gillies Hill

Castlehill Dun

The Biggest Limekiln

Bannock Burn

Sauchie Crag fort

North Third Reservoir

Lewis Hill

Spitfire crash site

0 500 2500

metres

The Direct Route: 3.5 m (5.60 km)

This route starts from the rough parking at the southern end of North Third Reservoir (*275606, 688032, 56° 04' 08" N 3° 59' 59" W*), however, you have several choices. You can walk round either the eastern or western side of the reservoir. The western side is flat with a path and bridges (though avoid short cuts through the mud). The eastern option has a climb up Lewis Hill, which has an uneven and muddy track, then walk around the eastern side of the reservoir, which opens some great views. Once you cross down into Windy Yett Glen (*276085, 689341, 56° 04' 51" N 3° 59' 34" W*), you have even more options. Once you have reached the dam itself and explored it, you have two choices of exit routes. The most obvious is to descend a curving stairway on the downstream face of the larger section of the dam, beside the overflow and fish ladder. A footpath leads north, away from the dam at that point, past the disused pump house on your left. It is now a private dwelling house. There is a gate across the private road just where it meets the public road. Turn right on the public road and follow it. The burn is to your right, out of sight in a deep overgrown gully during much of this part of your walk. After about 1.2 miles (2km) of road walking (the majority downhill) you again join up with the Bannock Burn at a flat concrete bridge on your right (*277065, 690745, 56° 05' 37" N 3° 58' 39" W*) at a place that used to be a ford. In our opinion, this is rather dull but is straightforward and easy.

There is an alternative off road track from the dam, leading to that same concrete bridge, 1.4 miles (2.3 km) from the dam. The burn is again out of sight for most of this route, although this time on your left. This route starts between the two separate sections of dam wall, nearer the east section of the dam. With your back to the water, lookout for an obvious foot path in the long grass (*275813, 689473, 56° 04' 55" N 3° 59' 50" W*), heading down to your right, at an angle from the dam and passing through a gap in an old disused metal fence. The footpath descends through a wooded area, crossing two small wooden bridges at the low point. After that it steadily rises on a wider, vehicle-like track. The Bannock Burn is out of sight during this stage, way down at the foot of a wooded valley to your left. The pump house, referred to in the first route, is clearly visible to your left, over the wooded valley just mentioned. A hundred yards or so before the metalled track you are on passes the end of the Sauchie Crag, which is high to your right at that point, you will see a small stone cairn on the left side of the track, (*276040, 689797, 56° 05' 05" N 3° 59' 37" W*). Leave the larger vehicle track at the cairn on your left and follow an obvious, narrow, walking track, descending into a wooded area. You are nearing the Bannock Burn again, you will hear it, still unseen. Keep going and as you get deeper into the wooded area and lower, it appears on your left, still a bit below you. This route is away from traffic and is a pleasant walk – it also lets you see more of the larger lime kilns we mentioned earlier as well as some of the mine entrances. There are also a series of other routes along the ridge of Sauchie Crag, which give you great views of Stirling and while they end up at Craigend, they take you further from the Bannock Burn, so we'll let you explore those on your own!

Lewis Hill: The magnificent Lewis Hill from the east.

How We Did It

Between the two of us we've done all the various routes over the years, and without any doubt North Third is a firm Cook family favourite. It's only ten minutes from Stirling and an absolute gem. For this, however, we went over Lewis Hill and then down by the pump house with a few diversions—as you shall see!

North Third: From Water Supply to Wild Fowl Haven

Your host is now cunningly changing direction from east to north east and finally north as it disgorges into the reservoir that lurks ahead. Your gaze at that point will be drawn to the previously mentioned Lewis Hill, protected on its west side by the steep one kilometre length of Sauchie Crag. An impressive escarpment of vertical cracks and folds, with its prehistoric fort perched high at the north corner. During the time of the lime workings, and for time immemorial before that, the Bannock Burn flowed, unhindered, below the face of that cliff, between it and a series of farms (including Townfoot, whose

An image of a goose in flight at North Third. Murray did photograph an osprey catching fish, but it was too blurry to use!

name comes from a small hamlet called Head Town which was to its west; so, the farm at the 'foot' of the town. As you follow the meander, the curving one kilometre stretch of the burn between the lime workings and the precipitous crag, keep your eyes peeled for the creatures you might happen across—depending on the season you are passing through, of course. They are many and varied, and include the flashing white rump of the wheatear. There was a time, because of that feature, these birds were more commonly known as 'white arse,' for obvious reasons. However that name reduced in popularity during prudish Victorian times. They are not alone and, as you pass, watch for ravens, geese, swallows storming, water ouzels dipping and perhaps you might just catch sight of flitting green-veined butterflies. Those of you who are in need of a break and get the chance to sit by the burn, watch for velia caprai, a rare version of the water cricket. Or perhaps even rarer: an osprey catching its lunch in the waters of North Third.

Shortly after crossing the road, you will encounter the most visible change in the Bannock Burn since those far-off lime extraction days. Just over a century ago, that symbiotic relationship between flowing burn and soaring crag was to be changed forever with the intervention of expanding industrialisation and similarly expanding populations. Not, however, as you might imagine, from the direction of nearby Stirling, but from another source.

The very rare velia caprai and a water forget-me-not.

That change you are about to encounter—the North Third Reservoir and the remarkable story it has to tell—lurks just a few hundred yards ahead, hiding behind scrubland and smaller trees. A concrete bridge, part of the early reservoir infrastructure,

A Cook family picnic on one of the islands in the middle of North Third.

like Kraken heads. Now, if you look you will struggle to find South or East or West Third, as the original name in the 18th century was North Rigg (or northern ploughed field), though how it got so garbled we've no idea! It no longer supplies water, and is currently a haven for wild waterfowl— as such, its shore is often covered in goose poo, though don't let that put you off. We have seen heron, the aforementioned geese, red kites and even (as mentioned) a hunting osprey catch its lunch. Also, stick to the paths, as there is some deep mud in places and people have had to be rescued by the police (though Murray's daughters got 'caught' in it twice and they seemed to enjoy it!).

takes you over the burn, after which a narrow path leads through dense bushes until you emerge on the shore of the reservoir with the crag now over to the right.

Before we get into its history, let us first sing North Third's praises. It's a great place for swimming, canoeing and jumping—watch out for the cold, though. As the level fluctuates in the reservoir, jagged bare rocky outcrops sometimes emerge from the water

Our source for the reservoir's history is Robert Porteous's book, *Grangemouth's Modern History*, and takes us to Grangemouth and a puddock. In the latter years of the 19th

Century, George Gillespie, the town bell ringer in Grangemouth, regularly warned local residents about water rationing—or worse, having the water supply temporarily cut off. The bustling port of Grangemouth, within the County of Stirlingshire, was growing and attracting new businesses, which in turn brought workers and an expanding population. The town was growing—as was the demand for fresh water.

About the same time, during a routine inspection of the Grangemouth water system, including an assessment of future demand and expansion, it was reported that a puddock (toad) had been found in a valve, causing it to fail. This was the last straw; a new water supply was an urgent necessity, and a search for a suitable alternative was directed.

In time, Grangemouth town council cast its eyes to a lonely burn that sprung from high on the northern flank of Earls Hill, in the Touch Hills, about 19 kilometers as the crow flies. This, our Bannock Burn, was identified as the most suitable contender to slake their thirst. Grangemouth Town Council then purchased the land required and developed it as a source of fresh water for the town, in order to build a reservoir around Shielbrae House, which was previously known as North Third. According to newspaper reports at the time, Stirling Town Council seemed less than delighted about a development that allowed

A pair of images from the construction of North Third, including the workers' accommodation where Daniel stayed. Images reproduced courtesy of Falkirk Community Trust.

the Burgh of Grangemouth to plunder 'their' water. However, despite Stirling's apparent disapprobation, the order was approved and in 1905 Grangemouth's Provost, A. Mackay, wielding a silver spade,[16] turned the first turf and the work to create a reservoir on the Bannock Burn was underway. It took six years, the earth embankment dam being completed in 1911, destining Townfoot Farm to the deep, in a reservoir covering some 134 acres of land. The dam wall comprises two separate constructed sections, built on either side of—and separated by—a large natural rock outcrop, effectively the third section of the dam.

Now, while much of this work was done by machine, much was also undertaken by hand by men called 'navvies'. These tended to be Irish immigrants who lived and worked on site. There are a number of pictures of the works ongoing, and of the men's accommodation—it was hard, dirty work. So of course, these navvies would want to stretch their legs and see other people, and they were in the habit of walking into Cambusbarron for a drink. One of these workers, Daniel Gallagher from County Donegal, was coming

back from the village and dropped down dead. He was found the next day, St Patrick's Day of 1907, and was buried on the spot. His grave is marked by a pile of stones which for decades after was added to as people walked past. We struggled to find the grave (276576, 691882; 56° 06′ 13″ N 3° 59′ 09″ W) and it took a few visits, though eventually Murray and his daughters were able to pay their respects and add a stone.[17]

Returning to North Third, what remains of Townfoot can be seen even to this day, when work is required on the dam and the water level is lowered enough. Indeed, Murray has swum out to there and walked along the now

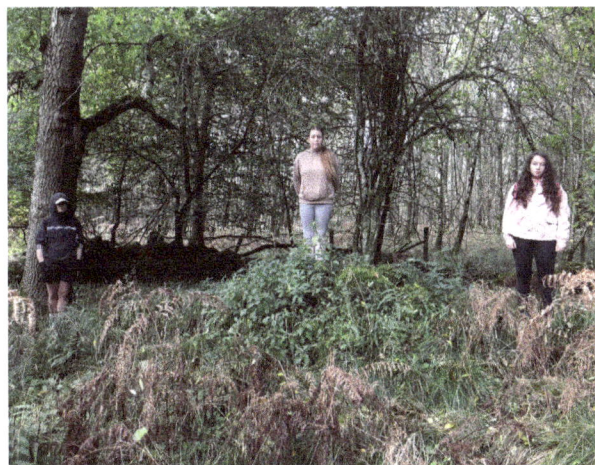

Murray's three daughters, Eilidh, Heather and Kirsty, across from Daniel's grave.

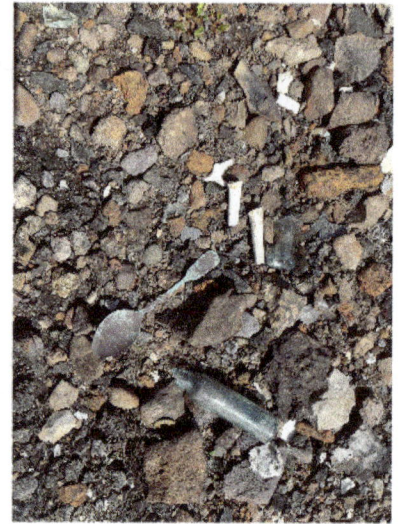

The drowned remains of Townfoot.

flooded road. Pottery recovered by Murray from the drowned fields around Townfoot suggest the farm was founded in the 17th century.

Returning to the opening of North Third, staff from the *Grangemouth Advertiser* were on hand to report the official party setting out to the opening in 1911. They assembled at the Borestone Flag, headed along the Sauchie Valley, over the Bannock Ford and up to their new water supply. It seems, from his poetic description, that the reporter was overcome with emotion when first setting eyes on North Third: 'On arrival they found water of the deepest blue, flecked by cloud and ruffled by winds from the west, flashing like silver pointed gems kissed by sunbeams.'

The deed was done and where, for centuries, the Bannock Burn had meandered untrammelled for around 14.5 miles (23.3 km) from its wellspring on the flank of Earl's Hill, to run its course and empty its contents into the River Forth—and in doing so, provide enough power to turn the mills of farms and the industry of townships it passed through— its free flow curbed forever, neutered by the North Third Reservoir dam.

GRANGEMOUTH TOWN COUNCIL AND OFFICIALS.

The formal opening of North Third including Grangemouth's Provost MacKay (centre) who turned the first turf.

However, while the Bannock Burn's natural flow was reduced, it did not die and it now shared its riches between two communities. Its outpouring now regulated and divided

The magnificent North Third Water Tower.

between an 18 inch diameter metal pipe providing much needed water to quench the thirst of Grangemouth's residents and industry, whilst the remainder continued to follow its ancient course to replenish the River Forth and farmlands en route.

A Fallen Hero
As we continued our walk, the ancient battle-axe still fresh in our thoughts, we came across a secret from a more recent conflict.

Just before the looming crags, a well-worn pathway snakes out in front of you, along the right bank of the burn. After no more than 80 yards or so from the tarred road, look over to your right. An old dry stone dyke and a line of three oak trees run parallel to your path, about forty yards or so from your position. Immediately beyond the dyke and the oak trees, there is an area of boggy ground. On the far side of the boggy area, the ground rises into a slope with a copse of beech trees. The Bannock Burn's next secret will now be revealed. In that bog, between the wall and the copse of beech trees, adjacent to the oak nearest the reservoir (275677, 688084, 56° 04'

The crash site and Ian leading a commemoration on the 79th Anniversary, 29th January 2021.

10″ N 3° 59′ 55″ W), is the spot where a Spitfire aircraft crashed during World War II and lay virtually undisturbed for some fifty-seven years. The pilot, a 37 year old Belgian national called Henri Jeanne Paul De La Bastita, was killed in that crash on 29th January 1943. His remains were recovered three days after the crash and buried locally, although the aircraft was left in situ.[18] In memory of brave Henri (and, indeed, all his fallen comrades), who gave his life for our freedom beside the Bannock Burn that day, allow us to cite what we know about that pilot and the history of the aeroplane he flew: Spitfire P8394, named *Gibraltar*.

Henri took part in initial pilot training between 30 September 1924 and his graduation as a Belgian fighter pilot on 15 January 1926. He joined the reserve in 1927 and was recalled to active duty during the mobilisation in September 1939. During the campaign of May 1940, against the German invasion of his country, he executed reconnaissance missions with 1st Squadron of the 1st Aeronautical Regiment in a Fairley Fox IIIC. On 14 May, during a reconnaissance mission over the Albert Canal in Belgium, his plane suffered a pierced fuel tank and he had to execute a crash landing. He was taken prisoner and spent some months of captivity at Oflag 4C, Colditz, Germany. He escaped from Colditz (quite how is at present unknown) and made his way to Britain, where he joined the RAF Voluntary Reserve[19] and signed up to fly Spitfires and continue his resistance of the German invasion and occupation of his country. European allies played a key role assisting the British, and between 1 June 1940 and 8 May 1945, 521 Belgian officers served as

The Spitfire Memorial at Grangemouth.

The Spitfire caught the attention of the British through the role it played during World War II, in particular when protecting the escape of the remnants of the defeated British and Allied armies in the summer of 1940 at Dunkirk, and also through its Battle of Britain exploits (the latter causing the Germans to put on hold their plans for an early invasion). Incidentally, the Hurricane aircraft actually shot down more enemy planes than the Spitfire, and more of them were destroyed with more aircrew killed. It made no difference —the Spitfire had seared itself into the psyche of the British people and gained iconic status.

pilots or navigators in the RAF. 128 (nearly one quarter) were killed.

During World War II, the skies over central Scotland buzzed with the sound of fighter aircraft. many were Spitfires from Grangemouth and its satellite base at Balado near Kinross, out of which pilots practiced their craft or tested their aeroplanes. Such activity brought occasional tragedy; sometimes aircraft developed faults, or a pilot in training made a fatal mistake.

From their first successful flight trials in 1936 until the end of the war, over 20,000 Spitfire aircraft were built. The design being altered as improvements were made and requirements were identified. As part of the war effort, many were built by money raised privately by individuals, companies or communities, with each purchaser having the naming rights.

In late 1940, the garrison and people of Gibraltar raised and donated £5,594, 11s, 3d for the construction of an aircraft. Spitfire P8394 was born.[20] It was named 'Gibraltar' in recognition of that donation. As with all such donations, the Ministry of Aircraft Production marked it by presenting to the donors two framed photographs of the built aircraft and a metal plaque, which says:

In the hour of peril, the people of Gibraltar earned the gratitude of the British Nation, sustaining the valour of the Royal Air Force and fortifying the cause of freedom, by the gift of a Spitfire Aircraft. "They shall mount up with wings as eagles."

Gibraltar had a busy service after first being built at Birmingham. It went to Kent and first flew over France in bomber escorts and sweeps. From there it went to Cornwall and then to Londonderry, then to Belfast and Cumbria before ending up at Balado Bridge, Kinross—a satellite to the main Grangemouth Base, where Henri is listed on the memorial.[21]

Its last flight, on the 29th of January 1943, was from Balado Bridge after 'homing' training, which necessitated flying at high altitude. Suddenly all contact was lost with *Gibraltar*. After a search lasting three days, the plane was located in boggy ground just to the south-east of North Third reservoir, near Stirling. Only the tail and a small section of the fuselage was visible. Henri was killed in the crash. The cause is thought to have been the pilot's oxygen feed icing up and starving him of oxygen—situation that would very quickly lead to him becoming unconscious. The aircraft was not removed at that time and was left submerged in the bog. *Gibraltar* had completed 345 flying hours.

Gibraltar's propeller; image courtesy of Campbell Chesterman.

28

In July 1991, after poring over maps and MOD reports of Scottish crash sites, Alan Leishman and other members of the Scotland West Aircraft Investigation Group carried out an exploratory dig in the area. Their research indicated, and found, some wing wreckage and various small items that obviously related to the crashed plane. The ground was too dangerous to carry out further exploration and continue their search, so they marked the spot, about three hundred yards or so south of the reservoir. They had found *Gibraltar*.

John Hunter from Dundonald Aviation Group applied to the MOD for a licence to recover the Spitfire and nine years later, on the 16th August 2000, they returned to the site—some 57 years after the fatal crash. Campbell Chesterman, a local historian in Stirling with a particular interest in Spitfire aircraft, teamed up with Alan Leishman and others from the Dundonald Aviation Group and, after gaining the permission of the land owner and seeking help from two local companies—the Ogilvie Group, who supplied a digger and driver and Tillhill Forestry who organised a forester to cut back

some trees and encroaching branches—they commenced the excavation of the aircraft.

After hours of tricky and dangerous work in up to fifteen feet of stinking mud and bog, they managed to lift clear much of the forward fuselage and tail section. Then they recovered the undercarriage, oxygen equipment, radios, cockpit equipment, armour plate, fuel tank, radiator, supercharger, Rolls Royce Merlin engine, crankshaft and finally the buckled, three bladed propeller, complete with its reduction gear. When the engine was lifted clear, after all these years buried in a bog, the oil was still running green.

The remains were initially removed to the Dundonald Aviation Museum in Ayrshire, where, after cleaning, they went on display. Some years later, the museum went out of business and the MOD License for *Gibraltar* was transferred to the Dumfries and Galloway Aviation Museum. But *Gibraltar* never got to Dumfries, however, as another organisation intervened and removed it from where it lay at Dundonald. There is some confusion as to how that happened. After some research, parts of *Gibraltar* were traced to enthusiasts in Falkirk and Grangemouth, where they are currently stored.

The 11 foot high propeller also has a tale to spin. In 2001, not long after the recovery, agreement was reached between Dundonald Aviation Group and Douglas Alexander to display the propeller at the 'T in the Park' Festival at Balado. Balado was, of course, where Gibraltar took its last flight. While 'T in the Park' ceased to exist as an event a few years ago, attempts by Dumfries and Galloway Aviation Museum to trace and recover the propeller have so far failed. Its fate is still a mystery and, in our opinion, is a scandal. In December 2020, Campbell Chesterman, out of respect for the sacrifice of Henri, gifted the few parts of the Spitfire he still possessed—including Henri's mask—to the Belgian Embassy in London.

The mask fragments are now in the possession of the Senior Aviators Association: The 'Vielles Tiges' of Belgian Aviation Royal Society, who are to display them in their clubhouse at La Maison des Ailes in Brussels. The Society eventually located members of the pilot's family, who kindly released some photographs of Henri and also provided a brief account of his military history. We, the authors of this book, thank all involved for their support, co-operation and kindness.

The Western Isles in Stirling?
As you climb, look behind you at this point, back to the narrow gorge carved out and shaped by the Bannock Burn over the

The view from Lewis Hill back up the Bannock Burn to Earl's Hill

centuries as it has gurgled through Swallowhaugh. Whilst not exactly the equivalent of the eye-catching splendour of some more famous Scottish glens and straths, it does not need to cower or apologise, for what it lacks in eye candy, it more than makes up for it in the story it has to tell about Scotland's past—from its geological history, complete with fossils, to its industrial past and role of the history of our country's working class and not forgetting its links to the peoples of the Bible lands and much more. So while at first glance this place, this shallow hollow, perhaps appears unremarkable, do not dismiss it; stop and 'look aboot ye'. You are in the presence of so many ancient connections, you are indeed in a truly remarkable place.

The path then winds its way up the crag. The woods are full of deer, and once Murray went up near dawn to watch the white tails of the deer flash and jump ahead of him as they tried to get away. There is a narrow strip between the woods and the cliff, frequently used by

The view to the north from Lewis Hill.

mountain bikers. If you near the Ordnance Survey triangulation point at the high point of the Sauchie Crag during the spring, there will be a golden hue from a crowd of daffodils clustered round the summit. North Third reservoir lies below and beyond a vast panorama to the west. As you scan the horizon you will see Ben Ledi, Ben Vorlich, Stuc a Chroin, Ben Chonzie, the Ochils and more.

Now, a wee aside about that name: 'Lewis Hill'. Is there a link to the Western Isles here? No, this looks like another garbled name. In the 18th century, there was a farm here called

North Third's islands and a very precipitous rock!

'Laws', and law is of course a Scots word for hill, so Laws should probably be Law's Farm which would have become Lewis.

The view from this ridge over North Third is the best way to grasp its beauty and scale. There are also some very precarious-looking rocks, the wind and rain slowly but surely weathering away the softer rock. In 2002, North Third ceased to be a public water supply and became a trout fishery, which eventually failed.

Warring Celts and Their Bling!
At the northern end of Lewis Hill, just before the precipitous descent through the wonderfully-named Windy Yett Glen ('yett' is Scots for gate), there is an ancient hillfort (276297, 689335, 56° 04′ 51″ N 3° 59′ 21″ W). It's difficult to spot, especially over the summer, when it's covered with bracken full of ticks!). The fort is built on a promontory and has a pair of enclosing banks, one of which crosses the path. We don't know precisely when this hillfort was built, but it seems to be one of a pair on either side of the Bannock Burn Valley. The other, on Gillies Hill (276867, 691763, 56° 06′ 10″ N 3° 58′ 52″ W), can be seen from this one and has been excavated. Gillies Hill was also built on a promontory and comprises three banks enclosing off the promontory, but it's completely covered in bracken. Excavations here in the 1980s dated the site to around 500 BC. This is roughly contemporary with the Blair Drummond magnificent golden Celtic torcs, with origins

in the Mediterranean found by a metal detectorist. Quite how they got into Scotland is unknown, but it does reveal there were always people worth a few quid in the area! After the fort, we began the slow descent down Windy Yett Glen heading to the dam —be warned, this path is very rough.

Art Deco Civic Pride
To get to the dam, follow the base of the cliffs along a rough path heading west. This takes you under a fence and through some conifers.

The dam is simply a wonder of engineering and civic pride, with incredible views to the north. The pier access bridge reveals the names of the long-dead politicians who commissioned the work but not, of course, of Daniel Gallagher or the other men who laboured at its construction. All of the ornamental metal proudly exclaims the manufacturer's name: A and J Main Co Ltd, Glasgow, London and Dublin, who worked across the Empire including Calcutta, Chittagong and Nairobi.[22]

No expense spared... some fabulous metal work.

For the last few years the water in the reservoir has been lowered while Scottish Water conducts repairs. This means more of the lost landscape is visible, and you are able to lie on the south-facing dam wall and soak up the heat from the sun-warmed stone. The water at this end can be noticeably warmer, and the rocky knoll is a good place to jump in if you want—but only when the levels are right. The north buttress face of the dam is like a massive manicured lawn. We resisted the temptation to roll down it and took the steep steps that take you to a cut track. Alongside the path, there are a few reminders of the early days of the dam and its original function. There are dome-shaped cast iron valve covers, with the letters GWW (Grangemouth Water Works) thereon.

The Pump House
Carrying along this road will take you to the aforementioned 1931 pump house, now a B listed building—and beyond it, on the same side of the path, you will see the original Engineer's House, built at the same time as the dam in 1905, using the same brick. Like the pump house, it is now also a private dwelling. There is a gate across the private road, just where it meets the public road.

Murray first visited the Pump House (275736, 689977, 56° 05′ 11″ N 3° 59′ 55″ W) when it had lain abandoned for decades, and it was certainly an eerie place. Ian went back himself when it had just been bought and was being converted. He got a tour of the interior, and witnessed a rather sad act of bureaucratic

From cutting edge vital service to ruin... the North Third Pump House.

34

The hooks for the board room... half have been taken away!]

vandalism where an original mosaic of Grangemouth burgh symbol was cut into to put a new door. Urggggh!

Ian and Murray were lucky enough to gain access to the Engineer's House, which contained a room the engineer could not use. Outside this forbidden room was a row of over two dozen coat hooks, which were only used one day of the year. When the Reservoir Board came to inspect the works, they hung their coats up and entered the locked room, and the engineer's wife kept them fed and watered as they pontificated. Eventually the whole complex was taken over by what became Scottish Water. The man in charge—Alasdair Tollemache, a lovely chap who became a Stirling Councillor—lived on site. It was Alasdair who gave us the tour of his house and, as he proudly exclaimed, he was the Englishman in charge of the Bannock Burn!

Romans, Celts and Empire

After the Engineer's House we carried on to the main road and turned right, following the road down the hill. Now, the next left is a wee diversion which Murray took on his own. This is a Ministry of Defence off-road training ground, used for both tank and live-fire practice. Within its grounds are the burnt-out remains of a military vehicle and heavy rutted tank tracks littered with spent shells, giving the impression you are walking through the aftermath of a military coup or a zombie apocalypse. And at its heart is the most incongruous archaeological site in Scotland (a bold statement indeed!). At the top of the training ground on a prominent rocky

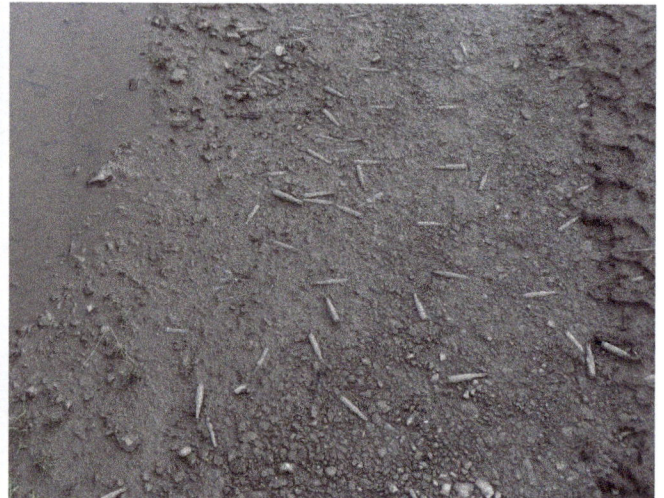

The MOD off-road training ground.

outcrop, dominating the valley to the south-west, protected from the tanks by both a fence and a sign saying 'Out of bounds beyond this point', is Castlehill Wood Dun (275075, 690906, 56° 05′ 40″ N 4° 00′ 35″ W). This is a broch-like structure, one of five in the valley, and amongst the densest concentrations of such sites in Scotland. Murray thinks this density is likely caused by the limestone, which will have created a fertile valley and led to richer farmers who expressed their wealth through elaborate architecture.

Now, if you know anything about brochs you may be thinking that this wee pile of stones

can't possibly be the same as the likes of Mousa in Shetland, but let us explain. So, in the past academics divided the many examples of roughly 2,000-year-old roundhouses with substantial walls found in Scotland into two categories of brochs and duns. The duns tended to be a bit more rubbish and were not always circular, while brochs always had staircases, cells and upper floors. Some argued that duns were not contemporary to brochs but a later form, though without much evidence. Other academics (notably Murray's old Professor, Dennis Harding) then suggested that given that brochs and duns have broadly similar

Castlehill Wood Dun from the Laws Hill fort.

Dun at the other (a bit like the difference between a stately home and a council flat), the variety of architectural form being related to time, resources and ability. The brochs and broch-like structures around Stirling are all the latest to be built in Scotland, and some of them are amongst the most shoddily ever constructed, as if they were being built without any real expertise. They also all seem to date to the 1st and 2nd centuries AD, with many associated with Roman finds and a majority of the excavated examples found to

structures and are found in the same area, they might well be contemporary. Perhaps an even more shocking theory—that brochs were in fact English!—was once proposed as late as 1971, suggesting they were constructed by migrants from the south who brought advanced technology and innovation; the clear implication being that duns were constructed by the locals as inferior replicas!

Current thinking now views the remains as a related range of structures, with Mousa at one end and things like Castlehill Wood

And the best preserved broch in Scotland... Mousa. Image by Sandy-Gerrard.

have been destroyed by fire. They seem to have been built during the Roman occupation of southern Scotland by communities that were trading with Rome, though crucially their architectures reflect a non-Roman identity, referring to both a 'free' past and a still 'free' north. The Forth Valley examples seem to have acted to facilitate trade and exchange with the Roman Empire. However, this was a tricky position to be in (think Vichy France under the Nazis); you were not Roman and the people to the north, who might have been your cousins, hated you as a quisling. Certainly, some of these sites around Stirling seem to have been destroyed by the Roman Empire (Leckie broch had a Roman ballista bolt recovered from its charred ruins). However, Murray thinks most of the sites were destroyed by their owners.

'What?' we hear you cry. Well, first let's expand on the Roman presence: between AD 79 and AD 100 the Romans built and occupied the Gask Ridge, which ran from Doune to the Tay and seems to have been intended as a temporary halt, but which became a boundary—the first ever constructed by the Roman Empire. The Romans then tried again with the Antonine Wall in the AD 140s, which was again abandoned after 20 years or so. During this period, southern Scotland was both a buffer zone between the Empire and the 'wild tribes' to the north and also a market for the hungry legionaries. This flow of goods to what was the biggest market in the world fundamentally changed Stirling's economy: people got rich—and dependent on that market. It's worth noting that like any good imperial occupier, the Romans kept the locals divided by shifting their favours and purchases, raising one local leader only to undermine them later. When the Romans finally retreated to Hadrian's Wall, the Stirling economy completely collapsed into a massive recession (think of the end of the mining industry). In response to this, the locals seem to have reacted by destroying the infrastructure associated with this trade—but rather than thinking of this as a riot, it's better understood as giving fleeting wealth back to the Gods.

But back to Castlehill Wood Dun, which was originally dug in 1955. This revealed an intriguing oval enclosure which contained

Roman objects dating to the 1st and 2nd centuries AD. The site was dug by Richard (Dick) Feachem of the Royal Commission on Ancient Monuments of Scotland (now part of Historic Environment Scotland), with a little extra help from Professor Stuart Piggott of Edinburgh University. These two Englishmen were giants of post-war Scottish archaeology and believed that sites needed to be dug to be understood (strangely enough, a controversial position today according to some in officialdom!). Both served in WWII and had relatively quiet service, but they were part of an archaeological generation which showed an overriding tendency to think of military conflict as a key factor in societal change. Feachem served with The Royal Naval Reserve in the Northern Isles and appears to have there encountered refugees fleeing the Nazi occupation of Norway.[23]

Murray thinks this experience may have coloured Feachem's interpretation of the site, which he describes rather negatively as probably containing 'huts and shelters... of wattle and daub', probably from 'scattered families, splinters from larger units dispersed by the effects of the Roman conquests in Gaul and Britain at the end of the 1st millennium B.C. and the start of the 1st A.D.' He goes on to say that these families and settlements were most likely destroyed around AD 139 as the Romans returned to build the Antonine Wall. Times have changed, however, and we would currently view Castlehill as an elite structure, occupied by someone of importance; probably a local chief of some kind who was liasing and exchanging things with the Romans. However, while we might quibble with his

One of the wall cells under excavation.

interpretation, we take our hats off to Dick Feachem; he produced mounds of data that we are still using today and without which we would considerably archaeologically poorer! Murray dug on the site in September 2020 and proved it was far more complex and significant—and dated to before the Roman invasion!

The reason we describe this site as so incongruous is that, 1,900 years ago, it lay at the edge of the Roman Empire and would have been visited by legionaries. It was at the frontier; a wild and barbaric place, full of smelly locals who didn't speak proper Latin, and who didn't want you there. It is of course now at the heart of a former empire, albeit one with a still global footprint, and it is used to train soldiers to fight in strange foreign places. To further add to the surreal nature, a structure which was built to be defensive is now protected by a fence and a sign! Mind you, both of these are needed; the excavation report from the 1950s notes a tank had recently driven over the site, and Murray's own excavations revealed soldiers had been using it for fox-hole training into the 1990s!

Some very large shell casings!

The route back down to the road gives you a brilliant view to Gillies Hill and the enormous hole punched into it from the quarry. Follow the road down the hill to Murrayshall Farm[24] (276630, 690832, 56° 05′ 39″ N 3° 59′ 05″ W). The mound to the right of the entrance is another of these broch-like structures—currently home to some very cute pigs!

Bigger and Better
We crossed the burn here to explore the almost castle-like line of three lime kilns (276554, 690683, 56° 05′ 35″ N 3° 59′ 09″ W) which are a minute or two back to your right.

These are examples of the periodic lime kilns we mentioned earlier and which date to either the late 18th or early 19th century, and were abandoned by around 1850. They are incredibly impressive and contain three 5m diameter kilns, 6m deep with a 35m wide frontage. Compare these to the scale of the clamp kilns we saw earlier in the upper Bannock Burn. There are smaller and older individual kilns and the odd mine or two further back towards North Third (276162, 690595, 56° 05′ 31″ N 3° 59′ 31″ W) if you had followed the path on the southern side of the burn. The ground here is all industrial waste from the quarries and lime kilns. The mine associated with these three giant kilns is 140m

behind them and while it's very obvious (there's a stream running out of it), please don't explore it or the kilns as they are all very unstable.

Now, we asked ourselves why these kilns were here and what had happened to the smaller clamp kilns. Well, you will remember our friend K.J.H. Mackay who wrote all about the Swallowhaugh's kilns. He explains that transporting the extracted burnt lime from the upper reaches of the Bannock Burn was not an easy task. In the case of Swallowhaugh, the most likely customers would be the nearby Sauchie estate and those a bit further afield, the Ochtertyre and Blair estates. In

Industrial splendour now in ruins: an 18th century lime kiln.

those days, circa 1700, there was little by way of manufactured roads. The area of the lime workings was really quite inaccessible, certainly for wagons and even horses with back loads. Another barrier to transportation, particularly to the Ochtertyre and Blair estates, was the River Forth and the difficulty of accessing ferry boats at the Drip, to the west of Stirling. However, the lime was good quality and much sought after, so—despite transport difficulties—it got though. Transportation, however, was a two-way process, as the fuel required to burn the lime, whether it be timber, coal or perhaps peat, first had to be sourced and then brought to the kilns.[25]

Periodic lime kilns are much more efficient than the earlier clamp kilns. They are permanent structures, mostly constructed of brick or stone, built a few layers deep for insulation. Like all lime kilns they require a source of heat. So central to the structure is a place for combustible material, usually timber. Small pieces of limestone are stacked above the heat source, normally in a dome shape. These kilns had room for one or two people to be inside at the early stage of the process, tending to the fire. It would eventually get too hot, and they had to exit the chamber and tend it from outside. The whole process would have taken a few days. There was a hole built towards the base of these kilns, and the extracted lime would be shovelled in there to cool prior to collecting.

What was it like being a lime miner? Mackay says the lime industry was seasonal and ran from April to November (sources are quiet about how miners coped over the winter), and in 1796 16 men were employed at 10 shillings a week (about £1 today) at this location. They used two horses for haulage, and annual production was 1,800 tones. Mackay has a more detailed account for the late 19th century:

'We started work at 6 a.m., and collected our tools from the smithy at the mine-entrance, where they had been resharpened. We had to buy our own dynamite from the store half-way between the mine and kilns. The working face was 3–4m wide and about 1.8m high. We drilled 4 holes across the face taking turns to hold the chisel or swing the hammer. When the holes were between 0.6m to 0.9m deep, we cleaned them out, put in some dynamite and a fuse, and plugged the hole with clay. We blew the charge after our break and filled the 'hutches' with lumps of limestone. A full hutch held about 15 cwt. They were run downhill to a lay-by using a 'snibble'[26] pushed through one of the 'biscuit-wheels' to slow the hutch down. We marked our hutches with our tally, and the pony-man took a 'rake' of them down to the entrance. We usually had the face clear by about three o'clock in the afternoon, and after that, went home.'

One assumes that injury and illness were a feature of such an industry.[27] Gathering evidence of such from these early days on the Bannock Burn has proved difficult; however, accessing more recent studies into the health hazards of working lime in arguably equivalent conditions has been less difficult. The following information was gleaned from a study into medical data from India. The top three ailments are as follows: eye disorders, 40%, respiratory disorders, 20%, followed by cardiovascular issues at 17%. The report does not cover physical injuries sustained whilst working. We have no reason to suppose the Bannock Burn workings would have been much different. It seems reasonable to conjecture that in addition to being exposed to illness and disease when working in this arena, physical injuries, particularly during the difficult transportation phase, may also have been a feature. As indicated earlier, it was not just beside the Bannock Burn that calcium oxide was extracted. It was and still is practiced, not just Scotland-wide, but all over the world and has been going on for centuries—and certainly before the Ochtertyre and Blair estates got involved.

We paused to think here: the valley behind us was an industrial area for over 200 years, billowing with smoke and the hustle and bustle of production; people worked in mines, burned and transported dangerous chemicals, polluted the water supply, suffered injuries and chemical burns, and led shortened lives because of it. It has all passed, the land has recovered, the water is clean and the kiln has fallen cold and silent, mute witness to a lost industry.

After the kilns we headed west. The path levels out here, and you find yourself walking through a picturesque wooded area with the Bannock Burn—pleasantly babbling along beside you on your left—giving not a clue to the bloodshed it would witness, a bit further on at some seven hundred years before. In pre-bridge days there was a ford at this spot, now replaced by an ugly but perfectly functional concrete slab. This is the ford referred to earlier, crossed by the dignitaries as they exited the Sauchie Valley route they travelled on their way to the official unveiling of the North Third dam in 1911.

* * *

Endnotes

16) The current whereabouts of which are unknown.

17) While we've put this story here, the grave is best approached further along our trail, albeit as a bit of a diversion.

18) After the war, Henri's remains were returned to his family in Brussels. He now lies in Row 3 of The Belgian Airmen's Field of Honour, Brussels Communal Cemetery. Memorial ID: 124656236.

19) The Royal Airforce dropped the title 'Voluntary Reserve' in 1943, a few months after Henri was killed. The reason given was that they, the RAF, thought the use of that term was divisive.

20) Technically a Mk 11A, which carried eight machine guns.

21) As a further WWII aside, North Third was the focus of a fake military base with lots of pretend tanks, used to fool the Germans into thinking Stirling Castle was to be the base of an invasion of Norway.

22) You can access one of their catalogues online at the Engine Shed in Stirling, and if you have a look I'm sure you will be able spot the North Third gates (please note they are no longer for sale!).

23) This is where the word 'quisling' comes from; Vikun Quisling was the Norwegian Prime Minster who collaborated with the Nazis.

24) Incidentally, the path to the west of Murrayshall Farm which takes you to Cambusbarron is the best approach to Daniel Gallagher's grave.

25) Irish folklore contains an interesting use for a lime-kiln; apparently, if you cast a ball of worsted into a lime-kiln then wind the loose end around your hands, the cast ball may be caught by an invisible hand. If that happens, you call out, 'Who holds the ball?' The answer will be the name of your future husband or wife. A warning: this experiment must be carried out only at midnight, in complete silence and when alone. We assume consuming poitín can help.

26) A 'snibble' in this context is a bar of wood or iron used as a brake to drag on a wagon, a bogey or a hutch in mining, particularly drift mining.

27) Indeed, it's worth noting that Stirling's Old Town Cemetery contains a 19th century monument to one Daniel Ferguson, a traditional Gaelic bone setter, which perhaps gives an indication of how common physical injuries were.

STAGE 3
WESTER CRAIGEND TO CALTROP PLACE

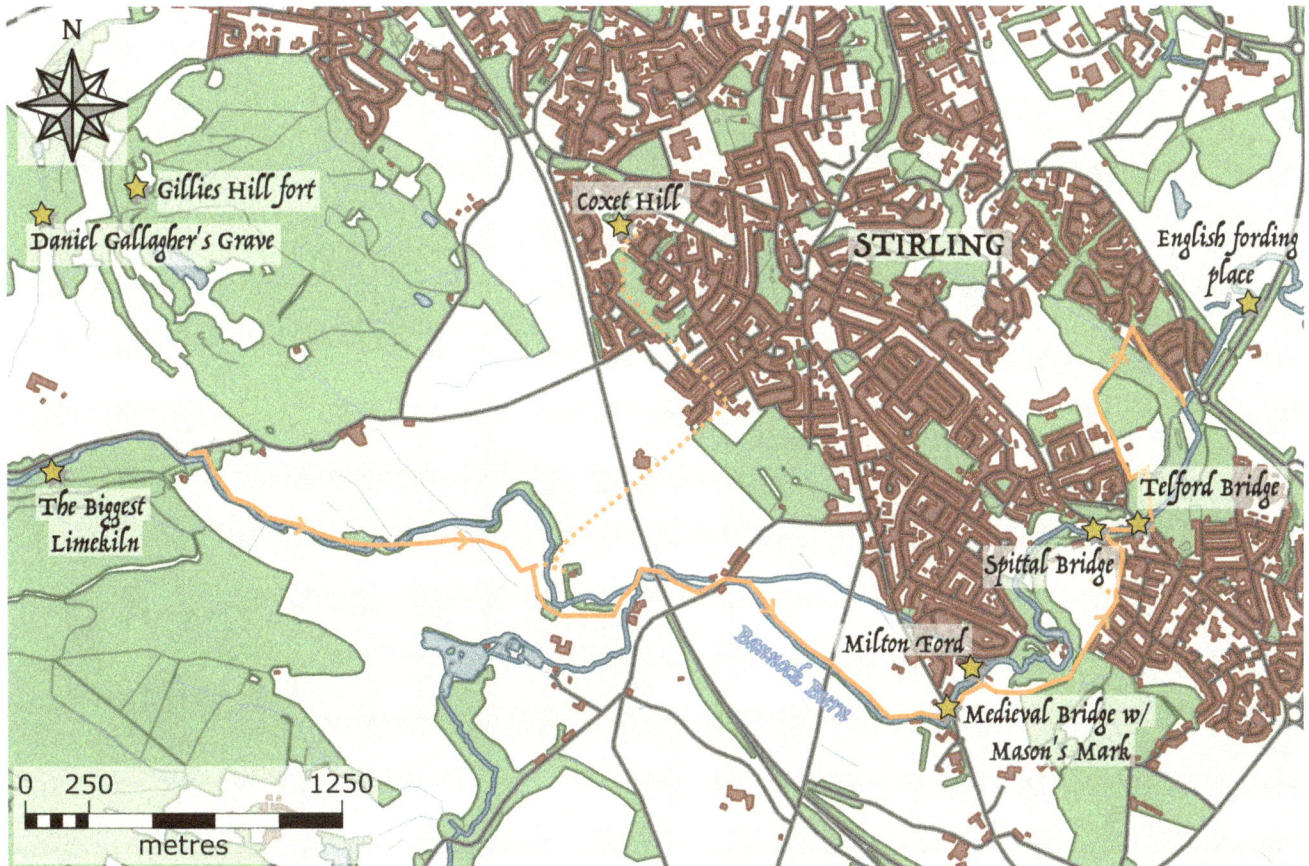

N

Gillies Hill fort

Daniel Gallagher's Grave

Coxet Hill

STIRLING

English fording place

The Biggest Limekiln

Telford Bridge

Spittal Bridge

Bannock Burn

Milton Ford

Medieval Bridge w/ Mason's Mark

0   250   1250

metres

The Direct Route: 4 miles (6.5 km)

As with Stage 2 there are options on the first bit of this walk, though both aim to take you to Chartershall. The most direct route takes you to the south of the burn across the concrete bridge along an untarred track. This ends up at Cultenhove and Swan's Fishery. Turn left at the end (*278760, 689742, 56° 05' 06" N 3° 57' 00" W*) and walk along the main road past Chartershall Farm and over the M9 to Chartershall (*278760, 689742, 56° 05' 06" N 3° 57' 00" W*). This is the boring route – though it will keep your feet dry and avoid some very curious cattle!

The alternative route follows the burn, heading up the hill from the Wester Craigend 'carpark' and its concrete bridge, take the first right and turn into the field (*277163, 690777, 56° 05' 38" N 3° 58' 34"W*) (it can be very muddy here), then turn right and start walking down the hill to the burn. The field here often has inquisitive cows in it, don't panic though and keep to the edge of the field next to the burn. There is a path and footbridge marked on the OS maps, but that's all gone now so you therefore have to ford the burn (*277982, 690427, 56° 05' 28" N 3° 57' 46" W*), there are lots of fences and not so many gates so lots of climbing and remember to cross at strainers. Keep following the burn on its southern bank and you will eventually come to Chartershall House, the entrance driveway of which straddles the burn. At this point you have a choice, you can either follow the road and cross the bridge over the motorway into Chartershall itself or you can walk down into the field (*278723, 690144, 56° 05' 19" N 3° 57' 02" W*) immediately to the east of Chartershall House, cross the burn and then scramble under the motorway bridge (very muddy but the thrum and wump of passing traffic is cool). At Chartershall, turn right after the two bridges (*278760, 689742, 56° 05' 06" N 3° 57' 00" W*) and again follow the burn, but not the lade. There is no path here and it can be quite muddy. To your left is Monument Hill, the core of the Bannockburn Visitor Centre. As you approach New Line Road (*279760, 690207, 56° 05' 22" N 3° 56' 03" W*), there are narrow gates/styles on both sides. Eventually you will come to the bridge at Milton (*280155, 689755, 56° 05' 08" N 3° 55' 39" W*), you can either go under this and scramble up the right bank or climb the dyke and cross the road.

Those cattle!

At this point there is a formal designated path to the right of the burn, which should be followed, keeping the burn to your left, until the large set of stairs (*280696, 689969, 6° 05' 15" N 3° 55' 08" W*). You can either turn left here and walk down to the burn and turn right at the bottom or turn right here and follow Coal Wynd, before turning left at its end – both end up at Spittal's Bridge. Cross Spittal's Bridge (*280760, 690447, 56° 05' 31" N 3° 55' 05" W*) and turn right towards the mill in the corner, then take the stairs to the right on the mill and climb up the Telford Bridge (*280943, 690470, 56° 05' 32" N 3° 54' 55" W*). At this point there are two more choices: cross the road and head down the other side of the bridge and follow the burn to the houses of Caltrop Place (*281121, 690956, 56° 05' 48" N 3° 54' 45" W*) or turn left along and head toward Balquidderock Wood (*280767, 690978, 56° 05' 48" N 3° 55' 06" W*): cross the bridge and take the first right into Firs Crescent. Follow the crescent until it becomes a path, St Mary's Primary School will be on your left and eventually you will come to the school's playing grounds with Balquidderock Wood directly in front of you, to the north. Walk towards the wood and follow the path down the slope before turning right at the bottom and ending up behind the houses of Caltrop Place (*281121, 690956, 56° 05' 48" N 3° 54' 45" W*).

How We Did It

We boldly followed the trickier second option which, whilst staying immediately beside the burn and offering a perhaps a more pleasing on the eye experience with deer, birds and trees, is however over farm land and can be very rough underfoot. As previously mentioned, you might be investigated here by extremely nosey and inquisitive cattle.

The very muddy field was frozen when Murray first walked this way and, while that made it easier in some ways, the frozen cattle hoof prints created a very uneven ground which he tripped, stumbled and slipped across. The second time he did the walk, it

Calm and wooded: the Bannock Burn, where Murray saw the kingfisher.

was early summer and he spotted an iridescent flash close to the water—a kingfisher. You simply can't find the words to describe the electric darting of this bird, so why bother when Manley-Hopkins did it so much better in 'As Kingfishers Catch Fire'? Don't try to understand this (Murray can't, and he's been trying for years)—just say it out loud and let the rhythm move you:

As kingfishers catch fire, dragonflies draw flame;
As tumbled over rim in roundy wells
Stones ring; like each tucked string tells, each hung bell's
Bow swung finds tongue to fling out broad its name.

The land here is calmer, more tamed. The burn has been canalised, bounded by boulders, kept in place; contained, but still vibrant and alive. The walking was flat and easy, though the fences caused Ian to pause every now and then as he struggled with wobbly strainers. The cows were our constant companions, curious for change in very boring flat fields. There are lots of rickety fences here, all tricky to climb, and we had to

The first lade on the Bannock Burn.

ford the burn—there is a bridge marked, but it's long gone.

Eventfully we arrived at a long, straight, damp ditch (278165, 690469, 56° 05′ 29″ N 3° 57′ 35″ W), blocking our way and cutting off the meander of our host. This is our first encounter with another part of the Bannock Burn's industrial heritage: mills and water power. As Kipling put it in 'Puck's Song':

See you our little mill that clacks,
So busy by the brook?
She has ground her corn and paid her tax
Ever since Domesday Book

This is the Park Mill lade, which is all that's left of the first mill on the Bannock Burn which was demolished in the 20th century. The mill is first recorded in the middle of the 18th century, and borrowed water from the burn to power its grinding. The name suggests a connection to the Medieval New Park of Stirling, which was probably established by Alexander III in the 1260s. (He's the one whose death led to the Wars of Independence. A rather impetuous chap, he famously went over a cliff in a storm while travelling to meet his new wife.)

The Bannock Burn, in this middle section, had been lined with mills of one kind or another for centuries, though the 19th century saw their number triple and, as we shall see, one in particular had a big impact on Scotland.

The majority of the mill buildings and infrastructure, long since redundant, were dismantled and removed during the 1960s, leaving only one or two recognisable features, but mostly hard-to-find archeological traces. Today only three survive as buildings and none as functioning mills, their millstones abandoned to sulk as garden ornaments. Did the damming of the Bannock Burn in 1911, to provide water for Grangemouth, with the resultant reduced water flow, have an adverse effect on the milling industry a few miles downstream? Or was it simply changes in fashion and the move to different clothing materials? What about the visible remains?

Millstones as garden ornaments at Milton.

But let's take a step back and explore water power. Flowing water provides the potential to create a sustainable source of power. Such possibility did not go unnoticed by our ancestors, and for centuries that power has been harnessed by humans and has played a vital role in industrial and agricultural development. The Bannock Burn had all the ingredients necessary to participate in that story.

How does one harness the kinetic energy of flowing water to turn the wheels of industry? The 'run of the mill' theory is simple: construct a wheel with paddles, place them into the flowing river or stream in a position so the water strikes them and propels the wheel in a circular motion. The axle of the wheel is linked to a series of gears, shafts and other mechanisms designed to drive the machinery within the mill, which turns a stone to grind the grain. Hey presto, the energy of the flowing water is harnessed for the use of humans.

But there are two problems, the first that mill stones get worn down and need to be replaced and also that water flow depends on the vagaries of the weather, certainly in Scotland. The wheel can be overwhelmed by too much flow one minute and not enough the next. A method of achieving control and sustainable consistency had to be found, and the wit of the ancients came up with an ingenious but simple solution: the weir.

A weir on a river is not a dam. Whilst perhaps giving the appearance of a dam, it differs in one important respect. A weir, unlike a conventional dam, allows water to freely flow over it, while—at the same time—creating an upstream pond. That simple concept of a weir and an upstream pond introduces the opportunity of controlling the flow of water to the waterwheel.

The method involves diverting the water from the artificially created pond along a ditch dug between the pond to the mill. Water is then allowed to flow along the channel. A gate, at the point the channel connects to the pond, allows the water flow to be regulated. The simple operation of opening and closing the gate allows that control. The channel is commonly referred to as a sluice and the gate, not surprisingly, a sluice gate. However, it is never that simple, and the Scottish term for such a channel is *lade*. Some old Scottish documents and maps refer to it as a *lead*. One may hear or read alternative names across the United Kingdom, such as flume, leat, head race, mill race or perhaps penstock. During the era of working mills on the Bannock Burn, this technology was abundant, with numerous weirs and lades—some shared by more than one mill.

In their earliest form, these mills mostly ground wheat, corn, barley and other forms of grain. Another early use was to power sawmills. Over the centuries they became more sophisticated and perhaps more complicated as their output developed to include the manufacture of vegetable oils, powering textile mills and more.

James J. Hoffmann's book *The Influence of Water Mills on Medieval Society* maps the history of water power across the world. First identified in in Egypt around 300 BC, the technology soon spread across Europe and by AD 1086 The Domesday Book of England recorded 6,000 water mills. In part the technology was spread by monastic orders, who used the technology to maximize food

The remains of the medieval mill at Stirling Bridge.

production. Stirling's oldest mill, the Bridge Mill, was fed by a 12th century lade, which still has water flowing in it today and is thought to have been constructed by Cambuskenneth Abbey.

Robert the Bruce's Forest
The wee single arched bridge (278536, 690329, 56° 05′ 25″ N 3° 57′ 14″ W) just after the Park Mill lade is an 18th century packhorse bridge, which was used to transport small quantities of goods across the country before the introduction of the turnpike roads. The path will take you to Coxet Hill (278966, 691514, 56°

The wonderful wee Bannock Burn pack bridge.

year old boundary of the wood on the north-east side (278888, 691756, 56° 06′ 11″ N 3° 56′ 56″ W). This boundary was later used as the Scottish army's camp during the Battle of Bannockburn in 1314. Murray excavated here in the summer of 2021 during the anniversary of the battle and uncovered the remains of a medieval road.

Close your eyes and imagine the volunteer army preparing for the greatest battle in Scottish history, about to face a larger and better equipped English army: can you smell the smoke from

06′ 04″ N 3° 56′ 51″ W), which if you have the time is well worth a little diversion. Coxet Hill is battered and bruised as it's had a housing estate plonked in its middle, although it is probably still the best preserved example of its kind in Britain. The wood was established by King Robert the Bruce in 1307 and was originally known as Kokishote. The hill was designed as a cockshot wood; a cruciform forest, in which nets are placed along the edge of the wood and beaters drove the game birds to the nets. There are still lines of oaks on the hill (the descendants of the originals), and you can trace the arc of the 700

The truncated remains of the medieval road, perhaps used by the Sma' Folk.

the camp fires, hear the songs, the fife and drum and the noise of nervous excitement? Can you see Bruce, sharing a bite or two, walking round comrades and followers, steadying nerves, discussing strategy. Was he frightened? What was playing on his mind? A man full of self-confidence, a violent military genius, it was his destiny to first free and then rule Scotland, to succeed where his grandfather had failed. But there remained a question over his rule; he was not the rightful king, that was his predecessor John Baliol. He had killed his way to the crown and been excommunicated, he had risked his soul to be here and had assembled his biggest ever army. But if he failed to win, what would Scotland do? Would these once-loyal patriots desert him? Would he end up like Wallace: hung, drawn and quartered by a brutal foreign tyrant? As if with Bruce in mind, Churchill puts it best: 'Success is not final, failure is not fatal: it is the courage to continue that counts'.

Returning back to the Bannock Burn, just before Chartershall House, the path becomes a road and there is a wonderful atmospheric and gnarled willow on the edge of the burn, its twisted, sinuous trunk an indication of old age. What tales could it tell us if we could hear it speak? After Chartershall House, we walked down the steep slope into a field with two horses, snickering and playing with us. The owner of the horses approached us suspiciously. Remember, while we have the right to roam, everyone must be treated with respect and their businesses depend on the land we happily tramp across. Anyway, apparently local kids had been leaving the gates open and

A wonderful ancient willow.

Some roe deer bums!

was built at the confluence with the Sauchie Burn.

The Charteris Hall, Nail-Making and Hawkie

The weir sits next to Chartershall Farm, which is all that remains of Chartershall or Charteris Hall, which was first recorded as a Barony held by Sir William Charteris before 1470. His rights included taking a stream to feed his mill through the lands of Sauchie, which is presumably the Sauchie Burn. The Charteris family came to Scotland with David I in the 12th century; many served with Bruce in the Wars of Independence, and the current head is the Early of Wemyss.

she wanted to know if we'd seen anything, as she was worried the horses would get onto the motorway. While we hadn't seen anything, let us reassure you that the horses are still there, happily cantering across the field, haughtily ignoring the roe deer that drink at the shallow ford (278753, 690169, 56° 05′ 20″ N 3° 57′ 01″ W).

We crossed at the ford in order to get to the mill weir, the first on the Bannock Burn, and then under the motorway bridge. The lade fed by the weir runs all the way to Milton, and

The first surviving weir on the Bannock Burn.

Charteris Hall[28] was destroyed in the late 18th century, and the only surviving illustration of it is the wee sketch on Pont's 16th century map which shows a castle with two towers within a big garden. The garden is first mapped on Roy's mid-18th century map, and appears to show a Saltire style garden. Elsewhere round these parts certain gardens were Union Jack shaped, which were very popular at the time and a way of demonstrating political allegiance after the Jacobite Rising of 1745 (the one in *Outlander*).

Before the Sauchie Burn joins its big brother, it runs through Howietoun Fishery, which was something of a world first. It was established by Sir James Ramsay-Gibson-Maitland, 4th Baronet of Barnton and Sauchie (try saying that after three pints), and opened in 1873 to prove that trout could be raised like any other farm animal. Sir James' experiments were incredibly successful, although at one point an earlier site flooded, the fish escaped and had to be rounded up! He won a series of awards including two gold medals in 1883 and 1885, at the International Fisheries Exhibition in Edinburgh. Perhaps his key achievement was to develop a method for the successful transport of large quantities of live fish eggs, which was so effective that they could be sent to New Zealand. Indeed, such was his reputation, he was known as

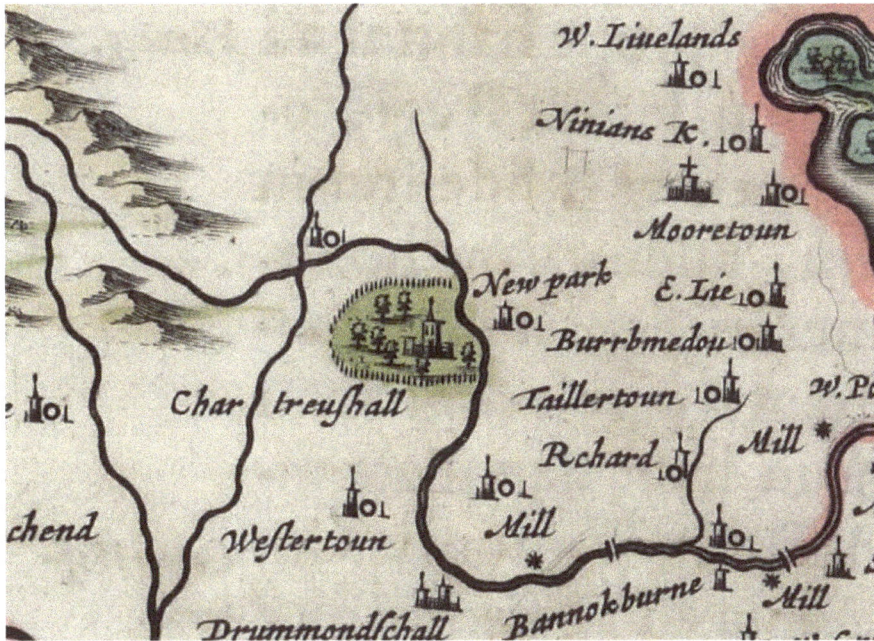

A detail from Blaue's 17th century map showing Chartershall; the only known image. Reproduced with the permission of the National Library of Scotland.

the Father of Aquaculture, and given how important this science is going to be to feed future generations it's incredible to know that its modern origins lie just up the road!

Now, lots of fish trapped in a fish pond is a magnet for poachers and the following anonymous ditty 'The Poachin' Gang' was composed in their honour:

Have ere you met the poachin' gang
That roams Steele Maitland's mony lands.
They take his pheasants, his rabbits and hares
an' even the trout in the burn tae spawn
are seldom safe frae the guddler's haun.

Then there's Rex, the poacher's dug',
on a Sunday morn' he wis hard tae catch,
wi' the first clang o' bells he wis aff like a shot,
up through the park tae meet the Dott.

On Sabbath morn they'd tak the road,
when kirk fowk gang tae worship God,
frae a' the airts o' the toon they'd gether,
tae rove thru' bracken, whin an' heather,
or being it wet, you'd fund them a'
spinnin' their yarns at Pirnha'.

There's Wull O'Hare, there's Jazz an' Dott,
A harem, scarem, boozy lot,

then Sean McCallum an Geordie Mair,
whaur could ye' get a thriftier pair,
an' ofttimes Penman jines in tae,
whit pranks an' larks they'll hae this dae.

Wi' weel shod shanks an' sticks an' a'
they'd wander past the auld Black Row,
an whaur the road forms aff a vee,
you'll find them sittin' bilin' tea,
in cans picked up oot the Lade,
enough tae start bubonic plague.

Big Duncan Don' he likes the fun,
he'd sit fur hours amang the sun,
an' up he'll gets tae say its nice,
av' got the Reveille an' ten slice.

They'd sit and while the hours awa'
an' heed nae, whit's the time of aw',
till Dott gets up wi' sprightly jig,
an sets the pace fur Carron brig,
an' there he gets richt fu' a' yull,
he an' his drouthie cronie, Wull.

These words I've penned are a' in jest,
as man tae man they ur the best
at gie'n ye tea an' breid an' cheese,
or walking ye tae yur knees.

Gin Sundays come an' Sundays go,
you'll always fund them sittin' there,
led by the King o' the Poachin' Gang,

the Gallant Wull O'Hare.

We climbed down and went under the motorway bridge (the eastern arch was dry when we went); there is a bit of a rough scramble on the other side to get up to the next field, and both of us got jagged by brambles. Ian's leg was very stiff by this point but he kept going—as it was all about to get much easier! But it's worth noting that the motorway runs right across the elaborate garden of Charteris Hall.

At the top of the field was Chartershall, the wee hamlet named after the house. In the 17th century this was the first road bridge over the Bannock Burn, built 1682. There are currently two bridges here, and the older one has an inscription stating that 'This bridge was rebuilt by the justices of the peace of Stirlingshire 1747'. However, this is not the 18th century bridge; this one was built in 1847 and the the date stone was preserved by Miss Maitland, a relative of the aforementioned Sir James. Next to the old bridge is a building with a date stone on the lintel: '17 W.F. 61'—this reveals that W.F. built or expanded the house in 1761. This is a curious building with a complex history. It is, in fact, the only surviving Nailer's Cottage in the area—a nailer was a nail-maker. In the 17th and 18th century, nails were made locally as the costs of transport were the key factor, and there was a thriving nail industry in the area.[29] The earliest record of nails being made was an order for William Lockhart, who was making nails for the Castle in 1633. John Harrison has estimated that 28,000 nails were made for just one roof, that of Cowanes Hospital, so you can imagine how many were needed for Stirling! We never managed to find the full name of the mysterious W.F., but perhaps one day we will. We'll return to nail-making further down the burn when we hit the core of the industry.

In the 19th century the building became a school, and there is a record of from 1872 of 48 children and two teachers[30] in it—that must have been a crowded classroom! We know that a local poet, David Taylor (known as the St Ninians Poet), gave singing lessons there, although he worked in a mill in Alva and was drowned while swimming. He seems to be completely unknown now, but one of my favourite works of his is *John Grieg and his*

Wig, which pokes fun at a poor bald man.[31] Intending to spend the day at a fair, John asked the local barber to spruce up his wig. The barber was delighted to receive such a commission and used honey to achieve a high glossy sheen, presumably because John was worth it! The result was of course predicable and very funny and for those without Scots this is best said aloud:

The day being sunny, the scent of the honey
Brocht bees, wasps, and flees, sma' and big,
An' when waffin' aff bummers, hale scores o'new-commers
Danced richt on the tap o' his wig
    A jig,
To the grief and dismay of John Grieg.

John ends up getting stung on the nose and starts running through the fair, causing chaos as he goes, although eventually he makes it home:

But after that John wad ne'er put a wig on
For fear o' the swarm o' the bees,
    And flees,
An' the wasps that did him tease.

Is there a moral here? If so, what is it—not to trust barbers, or simply not to be vain? But I hope you'll agree the poem is as funny as anything written by Burns.

Now, the most famous person to have gone to school in Chartershall was William Cameron, better known as Hawkie. William was a chapbook seller (cheap sensational tales of crime and ne'er do wells) on the streets of Glasgow, famous for his wit and comebacks. He became so well known that pottery models and a life size sculpture[32] were made of him.

He was born near Plean in 1784 and was injured as a child, giving him a life-long limp. He was clearly intelligent but, by his own account, doesn't ever appear to have settled down to anything, preferring life on the road. His biography, with the deliberately sensational title *Hawkie: The Life of a Gangrel*, was published over 30 years after his death, and it seems likely that it was edited to make everything seem worse. The text is meant to be both funny and act as a warning to avoid a life of sin, although its chief strength seems to be as a record of 19th century working class Scots. Murray read it and, while he doesn't

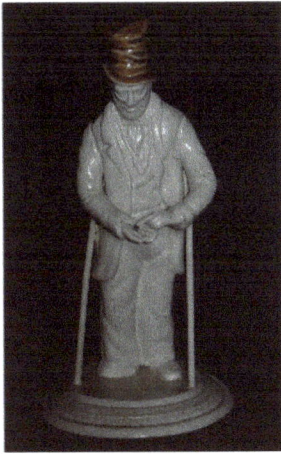

Three Hawkies for the price of one: the first is from life, and the second and third from the first....but the last has become a scandalous snarling stereotype from his 'autobiography'. The figurine was provided by George Haggerty.

want to come across as po-faced, doesn't consider it exactly *Oliver Twist*. Although it does feature pickpockets, rather it's a horrible tale of alcoholism, poverty and child prostitution, to name a few of the key points.

Battle, Borestone and de Bohun
After the bridge there is a turn to the right (279263, 690263, 56° 05′ 23″ N 3° 56′ 31″ W) and a right of way—our first on the route—but remember we followed the burn through the field, which is to the south of the path. We picked up pace here, as the ground was lovely and flat and it was very sunny. To our left is Monument Hill and the very impressive array

of structures and statues (the main one of which is called The Rotunda), celebrating Day 1 of the Battle of Bannockburn and the place where Bruce put up his standard, sitting in the middle of the Roman road, surrounded by pits dug to to restrict the English troops' movements, and awaited destiny. Absolutely fantastic: no visitor should ignore this great and atmospheric place. But—don't tell the National Trust—Murray's not sure it's true. All of this is based on the Borestone, a stone with a circular hole in which Bruce is supposed to have placed his standard. This became a tourist location in the 18th century, which was then visited by Burns who was so moved he wrote *Scots wa' Hae*, which raised the site's profile. The Ordnance Survey in the 1850s then mapped the line of the Roman Road running to the Borestone, and then the monuments followed. Murray personally thinks that the Roman Road is probably slightly further to the east, and that the Romans were not very likely to have run a road up the side of a small hill when they could have avoided it completely. The other thing to note is that all of this was a boggy area, drained in the 19th century (it's still called Milton Bog which is perhaps a clue so big that you don't need to be Sherlock Holmes to work it out!), and indeed—if further proof were required—the world's oldest curling stone fell through the ice here around 1511.

But what about the stone, we hear you splutter? Well, ask yourself—would the Bruce really have needed to drill a hole in just about the only piece of exposed bedrock in the area, when he could simply have planted his standard in the soil? Now remember that Bruce was amongst the sharpest of the tools in the box—so what do you think he did? But what then was the Borestone? Well, most

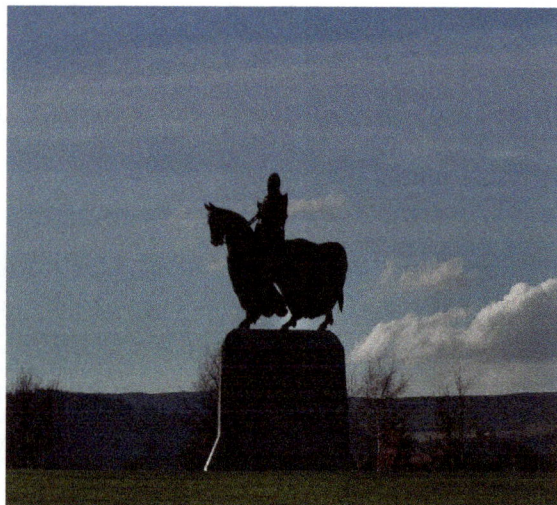

Monument Hill and the Rotunda, and a detail of the Bruce.

likely it was dropped rough-out for a millstone from the nearby Milton or perhaps even the New Park mill, though why no one came back for it is beyond us.

Now don't let us pour too much scorn over the Rotunda (though the NTS did manage to lose what was left of the Borestone!); it is still very atmospheric and when we walked on the low lying ground with the hill gently rising above us, Murray found he could envision the English army's confident approach across the open fields, and also began to picture the Scots' position: a bristling clump of spears several men deep, a spikey front that no horse would ever charge—the schiltron.

It's worth jumping back in time to look at the problems such a position faced. While Wallace won at Stirling Bridge where English incompetence and the River Forth helped, he lost at Falkirk a year later—mainly because the schiltron was static; it could not move. Indeed, famously Wallace roped them together. This meant that the English could surround them and block their movement while their archers riddled the Scots with cruel piercing arrows: a total and convincing defeat for the Scots. So, to avoid this trap, Bruce picked the battlefield and dug hundreds of pits to restrict the English army's movement, basically copying the Spartans at Thermopylae, with a little nod to the pits that Caesar dug during the Gallic Wars. He knew when and where they were coming and planned accordingly. The reason Bruce knew when and where they were coming was because of a challenge previously issued by Bruce that he was coming to get anyone in Scotland who wasn't on his side, i.e. a challenge to Edward II to back his allies[33] in Scotland. He then systematically reduced the English infrastructure in Scotland, ensuring they had to march from Dunbar to Stirling and thus stretch their supply lines and make the invasion that much harder and more expensive.

Now, while no one has ever found any of these pits, Murray thinks that the setting to the south and south-east of Monument Hill is as close as you're going to get to understanding Day 1. Of course, this means we can now talk about de Bohun; clearly the single greatest square go[34] in history. So, the English army in all its pomp and magnificence had arrived. Edward II had made camp on the high ground to our right (Croftside, but we'll come to that later), and the vanguard of less than half the English army approached the Scottish position—minus Edward, who did not want to demean himself by doing any actual fighting. Bruce had been caught slightly unaware; he was out front performing one last check, one final rallying of the troops. One of the English vanguard was a young knight, Sir Henry de Bohun, who—spotting that Bruce was on a wee small horse and armed with only an axe—charged. For Bruce, this required split-second decision making; he could easily have retreated behind his own lines, safe amongst comrades, but what would be the effect of that on morale? If he charged, he might lose and die, with Scotland's cause dissipating to nothing in the clammy cold mud.

De Bohun lowered his lance and began to gallop, the fate of a nation resting in his actions. At the last moment Bruce moved his mount to the side, stood up in his stirrups and hit de Bohun so hard that he split his helmet and head in two, as well as breaking the shaft of his axe. As de Bohun's corpse slumped in his saddle and his horse cantered off, Bruce turned to face cheering comrades, remarking that it was shame his favourite axe now needed repairing![35]

What about a little poetry? Walter Scott tends not to be read anymore as he's rather dated and a very high Tory, but there is a great rhythm to his account of the stand-off from *The Lord of The Isles*:

The axe-shaft, with its brazen clasp,
Was shivered to the gauntlet grasp.
Springs from the blow the startled horse,
Drops to the plain the lifeless corpse.
—first of that fatal field, how soon,
How sudden, fell the fierce de Boune!

This pretty much sets the tone for the rest of the day. The English keep trying and they fail, over and over again. Now, while this will inevitably warm the hearts of all Scots, it really wasn't a big deal for the English. The Scots threw everything they had at the English to stop them relieving the Castle—it took months of training and Scotland's greatest military genius to even simply pause the English advance. The English weren't really bothered; the bulk of the army had spent the day resting and watching events, a bit like a long day of cricket. They were in good humour and looking forward to round two, which they knew they would win as the Scots were tired and bloody—and tomorrow the English would try a different route to the Castle, one without pits, albeit muddier. So off they marched to their overnight camp between the Pelstream and the Bannock Burn, but more of that later.

Bruce and the victorious Scots retreated back to Coxet Hill to eat and drink, to count their losses, and briefly mourn fallen comrades. But they knew they hadn't really achieved anything—the English were still in control and the Scots were now tired. Did Bruce sleep that night? What was going through his mind? Could he even think, given the babble of advice he was receiving? Should he flee, or should they fight on? What did God think—was today proof that Bruce had been forgiven, or was he still heading to hell, dragging all of Scotland with him?

Whatever you think of Scotland's relationship with England and independence, we always think it is worth pausing at places like this to stop and consider the fallen, the bloodshed and treasure lost to control this tranquil field. But onwards ever onwards.

At New Line Road, or Longline as the locals call it (279668, 689911, 56° 05′ 12″ N 3° 56′ 07″ W), there is a wee climb to the road and a narrow gate and style on the other into Haughfield, though watch for the brambles as it's not used as much. You will pass between the burn flowing on your right and

Now closed forever: the entrance to Corbie Wood Stadium.

a full-size harness track with stables at the top of the field on the far side. While this is mainly used for training, once a year it becomes the venue for an important Scottish Harness Race meet. For years, the centre of Harness Racing in Scotland was at Corbie Wood[36] just a hop, skip and jump from Catcraig (which we'll come to).

When researching harness racing, Ian was happily asking about trotting and referred to Corbie Wood as a Pony Trotting stadium. He was soon corrected on three counts by local expert and competitor Gordon Allan. No, the majority of the harness racing at Corbie Wood Stadium, to give it its proper title, involves pacer horses, not trotting horses, nor are they ponies; they are Standardbred horses. The difference between trotting and pacing you may ask, as Ian did? Look at the legs, he was told. Gordon explained it this way:

Harness racing, or sulky racing as it is sometimes called, comprises a jockey sitting in a two wheeled cart, the sulky, while guiding the horse. The horses are either trotters or pacers, although it was mostly pacers at Corbie Wood. A trotter simultaneously moves diagonally paired legs. So when the back left leg moves, the front right leg moves at the same time in the same direction and vice versa—just like normal track racing horses. Pacer horses on the other hand (or is it leg?) have a different gait, sometimes known as a two-beat gait. The legs on the same side move in unison. Back left and front left move forward at the

Poetry in motion.... the thrill of the chase.
Picture courtesy of Donald MacDonald.

same time. This is also known as a lateral gait, as opposed to a trotter's diagonal gait. In the wild, there are two animals that move using the lateral pacer's gait: a camel and a giraffe.

Harness racing in Britain is controlled by the British Harness Racing Club. All the horses are Standardbred, the foundation bloodline of which can be traced to a horse foaled in England in 1780. It was called Messenger and belonged to the fabulously rich Astor family, who lent their name to the Waldorf Astoria hotel chain as well as donating to the New York public library. Messenger was relocated to the USA in 1788. Out of that sire line came Hambletonian 10, or Rysdyk's Hambletonian, foaled on the 5th of May 1849 at Sugar Loaf, New York. All official Standardbreds descend from Hambletonian, and are chipped and DNA tested to prove it.

To bring it back to its local origins, harness racing is centuries old and racing in this area, as far as we are aware, was held at Quarry Park, Raploch, in the early part of the

The Bannockburn Boxing Club.

twentieth century, then Bridgehaugh—where Stirling County now play rugby.[37] It moved again, in the early 1960s, to Corbie Wood—recognised as one of the premier tracks in Scotland.[38] As a side note, Corbie Wood is also home to Bannockburn Boxing Club and a very exuberant mural.

At the time of writing this account, however, harness racing in Stirling is over and Corbie Wood has been demolished. So as you can no longer visit, let us look back at past glories. The accolade for the most famous harness horse in Corbie Wood arguably lies between two pacers, who both raced in the 1960s and 1970s—Hurricane and Gay Gordon. Hurricane was probably the fastest pacer ever to race at Corbie Wood, whilst Gay Gordon was the most successful, certainly in terms of the amount of races won with over two hundred victories. A phenomenal amount, so much so that the achievement was recognised by the Monarch and a telegram was sent to Gay Gordon's owners, the Allan family from Cowie.[39]

Gay Gordon, a double gait horse which could trot and pace, traces its lineage back to a Swedish stallion, was raised in Orkney and purchased by the Allan family in the mid 1960s at a fair in Turriff. When brought to race in Central Scotland, its home was a specially-designed luxury stable built at Scotstoun Road, Cowie.

We hope you will forgive me on Corbie Wood, but we also spoke to Margaret Meiklejohn—whose family has a long and fascinating connection to the stadium, as well as trotting across the UK. Margaret and her twin sister Anne and other sister Louie (now deceased) regularly attended Corbie Wood trot to watch their father Alex, and their three brothers Alex, John and Wattie, train and race their horses there. Their brother Alex's son, also named Alex, has followed in their footsteps. After their father died in 2003, the family (minus their brother John, who sadly died in 2001), sponsored 'The Alex Thomson Memorial Race' annually for several years to honour his memory. The winner was given a trophy to keep for one year, and first, second and third horses all won prize money. After the trot was finished for the day, Alex, Anne and Margaret would put on some entertainment, as Alex had been in a band for years. Food was provided, and they all generally had a great night.

Now, the trophy that they won also has a tale to tell. The sibling's great uncle, William Thomson (Wullie) and his horse Sonny Boy had won races all over Scotland—including the Queen Victoria Diamond Jubilee Trophy at Thornton Games—outright. This trophy was put up in 1897 to commemorate the 60th year of the reign of Queen Victoria. Each year thereafter horses would race for the trophy and, as is tradition, it would be handed back the following year so that it could be presented to the next winner. It was promised that any owner who won the trophy with one of their horses on three consecutive occasions would be allowed to keep it. Their Great Uncle Wullie won the Trophy in 1938 with Ideal Prince, in 1939 with Mascot and for the 3rd time in 1946 with Sonny Boy, so the trophy was his! (The wins were consecutive, as the Thornton Games trot was suspended between 1940 and 1945 as a result of the Second World War.)

Moving forward to 2019, Margaret's nephew Alex won the famous Hurricane Pace Final at Musselburgh Races with his horse 'Crack Away Jack'. This race is hotly contested annually by horses from all over the UK and Ireland. It is said that the Musselburgh Hurricane Pace Final is 'The Grand National' of Harness Racing. It had long been a dream of their father's that one of the family's horses would win this race, and it's fair to say that the trotting fraternity from Bannockburn enjoyed the win almost as much as the family did. Anyway, the

same year the Thomsons held 'The Alex Thomson Memorial Final' at Corbie Wood and decided not only to present the winner with the race's trophy and prize money, but also to arrange to show the Queen Victoria Diamond Jubilee Trophy at the same event.

On the day of the Trot, a lovely old Bannockburn lady, Mrs Mig McKenzie—who was a great friend of the family—was, as usual, at the trot. She was very emotional when she saw the Queen Victoria Diamond

Corbiewood winners—from left to right: Alex Thomson, Mrs McKenzie, Mrs McKenzie's daughter Evelyn Hamilton, and Georgie Cardno. Courtesy of Margaret Meiklejohn.

Jubilee Trophy. What the family didn't realise was that her husband, Tam McKenzie, nicknamed 'The Rancher', was the driver of Ideal Prince the day it won the Queen Victoria Diamond Jubilee Trophy in 1938 for their Great Uncle Wullie, and she still had her husband's winner's medal. Margaret's brother Alex was amazed and arranged for a photographer to take a photo at Corbie Wood of himself, Mrs McKenzie, and Mrs McKenzie's daughter Evelyn Hamilton holding both the trophy and the winning driver's medal. The photograph took pride of place in Mrs McKenzie's house before she died.

Just as Margaret's Great Uncle Wullie's horse Sonny Boy was talked about for years within the family, and it's expected that Crackaway Jack winning the Hurricane Pace Final at Musselburgh in 2019 will also be the topic of much conversation in future, there is much more to discuss. The family also owned a second horse called Sonny Boy, which was a regular winner at Corbie Wood in the first decade of the millennium. Margaret's father, brothers and nephew won a significant number of races at Corbie Wood with their

The next generation: Sonny Boy winning Race 1 at Corbie Wood on 21st October 2007. Left to right, the driver William Greenhorn and his son, also William, and the three generations of Alex Thomson. Courtesy of Bob Dougal, Kilsyth.

horses over the years. Winners included Carronside Lass, Carronside Diamond, Rhyds Pearl, James Brown, Arts Dancer, Jericho Drift, Coalford Legend and Daddyofthemall.

At the eastern edge of the racing circuit it's clear that the city has arrived—there are houses and the hum of traffic. We decided to walk under the bridge (you will need wellies to do this), and made a series of intriguing discoveries. Now, while lots of people had been under the bridge, Murray was the first archaeologist and thus the first to understand what we were looking at. There are in fact five bridges here, the first of which is on Blaue's Map from the start of the book. Every time someone wished to make the bridge larger, they simply added a new bridge to the side—you can see the lines between them and also where the bridge just used the native bedrock. Across the stones of the older bridge are a series of small inscriptions: weird-looking, arcane symbols. So what exactly are they? These are mason's marks (now don't race ahead—they are nothing to do with the Masons, and there is no clue here to the Holy Grail, the Illuminati or Jack the Ripper!) They were used by stonemasons to determine who carved which stone and, while they tend to be associated with medieval buildings, they were used into the 17th and 18th centuries and even today some masons still mark their work. Now, we really should be able to tell who these masons were as James VI's Master of Works, William Schaw,[40] issued regulations in 1598 requiring masons to record their marks. Like lots of government legislation it seems to have been ignored. While we don't know anything about these marks, they could easily be medieval given the age of the bridge.

On the other side of the bridge there is scramble up the right hand bank with a very welcoming path at the top, and this next stage

Four bridges in one—and eight different mason marks!

is basically a walk in the park. Now, we do suggest you should do this, as this is the start of the Bannock Burn Gorge which played a very important role on Day 2 of the Battle of Bannockburn—as we will reveal! When we went it was full of sloes. Murray would like to be on the record as hating sloes; they are bitter and stoney, and the thorns are vicious with a tendency to lead to infected cuts. The only thing that makes them palatable is to drown them in sugar and alcohol—but why bother? You can do exactly the same thing with brambles, apples, plums and raspberries, all of which are warm, friendly fruits that like to be eaten. You are of course free to pick as many sloes as you want, but please don't ask Murray to help—he will however happily assist you with drinking the resultant gin if you're offering.

The Nail-Making Poet
At Chartershall we learnt that one of the main industries of the area was nail-making, and one of the thousands of people who worked in that trade was Alexander MacLachlan, who lived between 1816 and 1887 just along the road at Pirnhall. Who knows what he would've been doing today, but when he was alive his one choice was nail making, which we suppose was better than mining. Anyway, he wrote a nice wee poem called 'The Sil'er Burnie' which, given where he was born, must be about the Bannock Burn:

I lo'e the sil'er Burnie; how sweet its singing din,
As it gently winds alang by ilk fairy nook and linn;
How dear to me the little flower, that busk the bank sae braw,
O' the bonnie sil'er Burnie that wimples through the shaw!

As you might've guessed, most communities had a local nail-maker given the weight of the product and the poor state of the roads. Milton, beside the Bannock Burn, was no different.

Early evidence of nail-making in the British Isles can be traced to the Roman occupation of two thousand years ago. The Romans employed blacksmiths in the 'fabrica' of their camps, to manufacture many things, including nails. It seems that seven tons of nails were buried in enormous pits by the occupying Romans when they abandoned their fortress at Inchtuthil in Perthshire. This may seem strange, but these sharp, thick iron points would've made excellent weapons to be thrown back at the Romans, so they had to be disposed of in the correct manner.

Like today, nails came in different forms depending on what each was required for. Some of the names for nails are intriguing and here is but a sample: rose, spring, sprigg, flat point, slate, spike, clasp head, jacket, tenter hook and box nails. Each took a different form as required for a particular purpose, and some of these names still exist.

An old trade directory of the Stirling area, from over one hundred years ago, mentions four nail makers located in Whins of Milton. One of those names was Jaffray,[41] which reappears over one hundred years later—still connected to nail making!

Carron Ironworks in nearby Falkirk seem to have made inroads into the nail business in the mid to late 17th century by increasing their sale of iron rods—their ledgers reference nailers in Bannockburn and St Ninians. However naileries were prolific long before Carron Ironworks got into the market. The requirement for nails was widespread, and particularly crucial to the building trade. Prior to Carron Ironworks' foray into the business, the hammermen of Stirling seem to have been a major supplier of the raw material to nail manufacturers.

The hamlets of Bannockburn, St Ninians, Whins of Milton and Chartershall are all mentioned as having naileries. As we heard

The Symbol of the Stirling Hammermen.

earlier, nails were being made in Bannockburn for the Castle since at least 1633.[42] The cottage industry of nail-making typically took place either within the nailer's house or perhaps in an adjacent outhouse-like space (like the one in Chartershall). It would be normal for nailers to provide their own tools and equipment; bellows, sharpening tools, and an anvil or a block. For the manufacture of large nails, a work bench with treadle-operated hammers was used to beat metal into various shapes. In fact it could even be as simple as a sledge hammer hinged to a post by its handle and an arrangement of ropes to raise it. In the midlands of England, that bench with treadle hammers was called the Oliver after the name of the manufacturer of such equipment—a bit like calling a vacuum cleaner a Hoover. While we don't know if the Oliver was used in Bannockburn, it seems likely.

All of this sounds rather pleasant; a little cottage industry on the banks of the Bannock Burn. No commute, local products and artisans. The truth is far darker. Like most industries during the 18th and early 19th centuries, nail-making employed child labour. We have figures for the nail trade, in which children as young as seven or eight worked from 6am to 10pm or 11pm, and were expected to produce up to 1,250 nails a day.

To add even more detail, the following is an extract from a Midland Mining Commission report dated 1843, describing a typical English nail makers cottage:

'The best forges are little brick shops of about 3.6m by 4.5m in which seven or eight individuals constantly work together with no ventilation except the door and two slits, a loop-hole in the wall. The majority of these workplaces are very much smaller and filthy dirty and on looking in upon one of them when the fire is not lighted presents the appearance of a dilapidated coal-hole. In the dirty den there are commonly at work, a man and his wife and daughter, with a boy or girl hired by the year. Sometimes the wife carries on the forge with the aid of the children. The filthiness of the ground, the half-ragged, half-naked, unwashed persons at work, and the hot smoke, ashes, water and clouds of dust are really dreadful. It was normally the nail-master who supplied the bellows and forge whilst the nailer supplied and maintained his own bench and tools. Iron was supplied in

6olb lots and taken home with the order. Once completed, the work was returned to the middlemen (known as foggers), these people were notorious for treating the nailers badly. Underhand practices were common, the most common was to tamper with the scales to reduce the amount of money owed to the nailer and they gave little allowance for waste.'

It was not therefore surprising that, in 1845, two hundred nail makers from Camelon and St Ninians withdrew their labour and came out on strike. Three years before, in 1842, striking nail-makers from the Birmingham area of England received financial support from their Scottish colleagues to the tune of £40. When the Scottish nail makers withdrew their labour, they appealed to their English colleagues for help. We have no record whether the appeal was answered but would like to think it was. We've included a copy of the letter that appeared in the *Northern Star*, a Birmingham newspaper, dated 21 June 1845, carrying the Scottish nail-makers' appeal for help. The same appeal also appeared in the *Leeds General Advertiser*:

'Nailmakers' Strike, Scotland—We have received an address, signed Alexander Davie, on behalf of the turnout nailmakers of Camelon and St Ninians, near Stirling. With one exception, an address precisely similar appeared in last week's Star. The exception is, that in appealing to the English nailmakers, the writer reminds the Belper nailers that on a former occasion they received in their support about £40 from the men now on strike. We hope our friends, the English nailmakers, will respond to the appeal of their Scotch brethren, two hundred of whom are on strike. All communications must be addressed to Mr James Jenkins, nailer, Bannockburn Road, St Ninians, near Stirling, Scotland.'

Evidence that, nearly two centuries ago, working people from both sides of the border were capable of entering into an *entente cordiale* in support of each other.

A little aside: many workers at Carron Ironworks were brought up from industrial areas of England, including nail-makers. It turned out that many of these workers were Freemasons, which—as we heard—has local roots. Whilst most joined the nearby Lodge in Falkirk, some got together and opened up a new Masonic Lodge within the ironworks itself. The inaugural meeting of Carron Lodge 138 (later changed to 139), in 1767, was held within the Manager's Parlour in the foundry nailery.

Let's conclude this brief foray on nail-making on the banks of the Bannock Burn by including an anonymous poem, 'The Nail Maker's Strike', written around 1842, at the time of an industrial dispute involving nail makers from Bromsgrove, just south of Birmingham:

Oh, you nail makers all that day remember well,
The last strike of which this tale I tell,
How cold and hungry we that heavy day,
To Bromsgrove Town did take our toilsome way,
And these nail forgers, miserable souls,
Will not forget the givers of the cause,
Nail masters are hard-hearted viles,
And the way we took was 13 miles.

Oh, the slaves abroad in the sugar cane,
Find plenty to help and pity their pain,
But the slaves at home in the mine or fire,
Have plenty to pity but none to admire,

Now, I wish I could see all nail dealers,
Draw such a load as did we poor nailers,
And see such punishment and such smarts,
That it might soften their hard stoney hearts.
Oh, you nail makers all that day remember well,
The last strike of which this tale I tell,
How cold and hungry we that heavy day,
To Bromsgrove Town did take our toilsome way.

The Grand Sweep of History Over Such a Wee Trickle!
After a pleasant short amble along the sil'er burnie, you will come to ford and a footbridge (279668, 689911, 56° 05′ 12″ N 3° 56′ 07″ W) and this, gentle reader, is where the inspiration for this book came from. We sat here for a

The most important ford in Scottish history?

wee while and just thought. Between the footbridge and the one we came under is the place where everyone crossed, from the Romans to the current Queen. The weight of history here is incredible, and absolutely awe-inspiring. To list just a few of those who crossed here: Agricola, Roman Emperor Septimius Severus, Kenneth McAlpine, various Angles and Vikings, William the Conqueror, St Margaret, Edward I, William Wallace, Robert the Bruce, Edward II, David II, Robert II, James I, James II, James II, James IV, James V, Mary Queen of Scots, James VI, condemned witches, Oliver Cromwell, Bonnie Prince Charlie, Robert Burns, William Wordsworth, Robert Louis Stevenson, over 100 million head[43] of cattle and many, many more! This is also where de Bohun crossed once on horseback (but only his corpse came back), and where King James III of Scotland is reputed to have been fatally injured. Basically, anyone and everyone who travelled north or south by foot crossed here.

This of course presents us with a problem: which stories to pick? But first, a wee detour across the bridge and into Milton.

Milton and Medieval Fake News
We have now entered the core of Milton. The 1862 Ordnance Survey map of this area shows five separate mills in Milton. Two woollen mills, a flour mill, a corn mill and the historic Beaton's Mill, the latter adjacent to the ancient ford that marked one of the main and ancient crossing points on the Bannock Burn. Incidentally, Timothy Pont's 16th century map also indicates a mill in this area. A milton is defined as buildings comprising a mill, the farm adjacent to a mill and tenanted by a miller, or a hamlet that has grown up around a mill. So with five mills, we have to assume that Milton was well named. An old Scottish version of Milton would be Milntoun.

The other Milton Mill: the first one is pictured above with the millstones as ornaments.

Beaton's Mill before and during the fire, the latter provided by Mr William Muirhead.

Only two of these mill buildings presently exist. Interestingly, both claim the same name, Milton Mill. Let us begin with the Milton Mill designated by Historic Environment Scotland as a B listed building (280150, 689995, 56° 05′ 16″ N 3° 55′ 40″ W), so as to avoid confusion. The mill referred to by them is situated in Collier's Way, Milton. While the mill has now been tastefully converted to residential use, it internally retains some of the original mill features; the water wheel, the lade and some of the internal mill mechanism.

In 1984, the Scottish Industrial Archaeology Survey described Milton Mill as being one of the best-preserved industrial buildings in the area, and it is thought to be the only remaining corn mill in the Stirlingshire area that still retains its machinery, lade and mill wheel. It ceased milling oats in the 1930s and finally, having produced animal foodstuffs for a while, closed its doors in the 1970s. Interestingly, locals refer to the mill just described as Milton Corn Mill. The other redundant mill building still existing in Milton sports a sign on the gate indicating that it is called 'Milton Mill', and is referred to by locals as simply Milton Mill. It was a flour mill. This latter mill, which is not a listed building, lies on the north bank of the Bannock Burn, (280150, 689995, 56° 05′ 16″ N 3° 55′ 40″ W), just east of where Beaton's Mill once stood.

It had used water wheel technology for centuries. However in the middle of the twentieth century the then-owner, an enterprising engineer, was aware of changing milling technology. The traditional water wheel was being superseded by a modern and more efficient solution, the water turbine. A method that involves channelling water from the lade into a pipe set directly above the turbine, the water is then discharged vertically onto the turbine blades, creating a more efficient transfer of energy to the mill mechanism than was achieved by the simple horizontal flow to a water wheel. So, in the 1940s, the traditional mill wheel at this Milton Mill was replaced by a turbine. The mill ceased working in the traditional sense sometime in the 1960s, rendering the turbine redundant.

That mill building is one of a very few remaining on the Bannock Burn—although no longer a working mill, and now just a house. The Milton Lade that begins its journey just upstream from Chartershall, flowing through centuries of history— creating clothing, foodstuffs and employment—continues to flow. However, the wheels it turned have gone. The lade empties its unengaged energy directly into the Bannock Burn beside this mill: the 'turbine' mill. If you look closely when passing this mill you can still see the circular outline of the water wheel, engraved forever on the east gable; a visual reminder of the days of the great mills. The turbine was removed earlier this century and installed in a mill at Ashfield on the Allan Water, to the north-west of Dunblane.

The other mill that gets talked about in this area is Beaton's Mill (or Beatoun's Mill), where according to tradition King James III of Scotland was killed following a battle with his son, the future James IV of Scotland.[44]

It raises as many questions as answers. Who was Beaton? Was it even a mill? Was James III really murdered there in 1488? Let's start with the king. As you all know, history is written by the winners—except, of course, when it's not written at all. On June 11th 1488, King James III—born in Stirling—died somewhere close to us after failing to stop a coup launched by his son, the future James IV. The official Scottish Government record simply states more or less 'on this day the late King fell at the field of Bannockburn'. (The king is dead, long live the king!) James IV's guilt at his role in his father's death led to a glorious age for Stirling, as he invested in the Castle, building Scotland's largest Great Hall and the massive monumental gateway; reorganised the Royal Park; re-endowed Cambuskenneth Abbey as a suitable mausoleum for his dad; invited new religious orders; built Europe's biggest ship; and conducted research into flight.

Anyway, this notable absence of information on the former King's death provided an opportunity for a bit of fake news. James III and James IV were both Catholic, but by the late 1500s Scotland had become Protestant—a process called the Reformation. Now, it is a little difficult to understand precisely what the problem was. Certainly the Catholic Church had become corrupt, and having the Bible in English rather than Latin seems like a sensible idea. However, in essence, as the Pope is head of the Catholic Church, this means that Catholics could be perceived as being loyal to the Pope instead of to the state, and were often accused of being underhand

—all nonsense, of course. However, this was the context for Lindsay of Pitscottie's account, which states that James III fled the battle and arrived at the ford, where he was startled by someone getting water, falling from his horse and stumbling to a nearby cottage. He knocked on the door and when asked who he was replied: 'This morning I was your King'. The people in the cottage summoned a priest (or perhaps someone pretending to be a priest), who pulled a knife and stabbed the king in his bed! A very poor bedside manner indeed! Anyway, the attempted point of this fake news was three-fold: to paint James III as a coward and absolve James IV, because in fact it was really all the fault of 'those nasty Catholics'. In terms of the question of who Beaton was, some suggest—with little evidence—that perhaps it refers to Cardinal Beaton, who became Chancellor of Scotland in 1543, three years before he was murdered in St Andrews. At that time the church owned much of the land in the Stirling area, and that speculation suggests that he is the Beaton of Beaton's Mill. However, the evidence for connection seems no stronger than the shared name.

Adding to the mystery, Historic Environment Scotland, in their Battlefield Inventory entry for the Battle of Sauchieburn, note that the mill contained a corbel[45] marked with the date 1667—so it couldn't possibly be connected to the battle as it wasn't old enough. The Royal Commission on Ancient and Historical Monuments of Scotland described the building as a simple 17th to early 18th century single storey cottage with a thatched roof. Unfortunately Beaton's Mill was vandalised and badly damaged by fire in the 1950s and demolished shortly afterwards, so we can no longer check ourselves.

To return to the final question: was Beaton's Mill ever a mill? The big problem is, how could it be a mill if it's not fed by a lade? However, some 19th century accounts suggest that the cottage was used as a nailery in the 19th century. A secondary meaning of 'mill' is a building used for manufacturing, so it seems it could well have been a mill of a kind after all. Local tradition suggest that in addition to manufacturing nails, it was a

Hielan' coos to the south of Stirling.

family home and also a visitor attraction, with the nailer willing to show visitors into the cottage to observe his trade. It is not recorded whether he charged a fee for such service, or if he was called Beaton!

Drunk Droving

So, we hope you are ready for another tale. Linger by the ford, take a break, have a bite of your rations for the day and let your imagination summon all of those cattle tramping and mooing through across the ford in the 17th and 18th centuries. You are at an important spot in both Scotland's economic history and the development of today's language. We refer to the cattle trade and, in particular, Black Cattle on their way to market.

There were several cattle markets, sometimes called fairs, located across Scotland. Locally there were such fairs at Stirling and nearby at Newmarket, Falkirk. One of the biggest of these times was at Crieff. However, the autumn cattle fair of the Tryst at Larbert that came along a bit later was undoubtedly one of the busiest. As you'll remember: if you wanted to go south at the time you had to go through Stirling.

The cattle's ultimate destination was to buyers in the south, mostly England. In these days, despite some 'encounters' between Scotland and England, things were changing. During the 17th century, cross-border trade was improving, particularly trade involving cattle. It was kind of one-way, however, with most of it heading south. The scale of this trade cannot be underestimated, and it's said that in 1663 nineteen thousand cattle were counted passing south through Carlisle. It

has also been said that during that time, Scotland was regarded as a grazing field for England. The majority of these cattle were heading for North Yorkshire and Norfolk. There they would be fed and fattened and sold on again, eventually to feed the expanding towns and cities of England, as well as the military, and were an essential commodity in feeding those who were expanding the British Empire.

Scottish cattle in these days were predominately Black Cattle. The term Black Cattle then described all cattle, and it is likely that the origin of the breed lies at the dawn of agriculture nearly 6,000 years ago. The term 'cattle' is interesting and given that so much wealth was involved in livestock they became known as chattels, a word used to this day in a legal context when referring to one's goods and chattels. Late Latin, a form of Latin used in the Roman Empire, used 'capitale' to mean property. In Old French the word 'chatel' meant the same, whereas the Old North French word for property was 'cattle'.

But back to Scotland. With all livestock being called cattle and the bovine becoming the most expensive and increasingly the most financially important element of a crofter's moveable property, the need to label that possession differently from the others became important. So, the predominant colour became the identifier and the bovine became black chattel, or Black Cattle. These ancient beasts were a lot smaller than most of today's breeds: about two hundred and fifty kilograms (for the more mature reader, that is about five hundredweight). They were hardy beasts, able to walk for days and weeks through the Scottish Highlands to the markets in the south. That lasted for many years; however, from the early 19th century the popularity of Black Cattle waned as developments in this field saw the emergence of many more profitable breeds.

So, the next time you stop to gaze at or photograph that iconic tourist favourite of Scotland, the Heilan' Coo, be amazed, because you are looking at the descendants of Black Cattle, with ancestry linked through hundreds of years of Scottish history, right back to the earliest times. Before moving on from tales of ancient cattle, let us talk about one of the persons charged with taking care of the cattle during the drove. John McMartin was a cattle drover from the Loch Lochy area north of Fort William in the Great Glen. As a drover he would cover hundreds of Scottish miles, moving Black Cattle to and from fairs and markets throughout the country. Sometime in 1752 he was involved in driving a herd from a place called Gallachie, fifty miles or so beyond Inverness, to be sold at Stirling market. Drovers had to stay with the cattle and often would sleep out in the open, wrapped in a plaid. For much of the journey, the staple diet of the drover would be some kind of gruel—typically barley or oats, usually boiled in water. One assumes there might even be some kind of meat carried to supplement the meal.

Whatever he dined on, he did get to Stirling and seemed to have had a successful sale. Instead of heading straight home, however, he tarried at the Fair for long enough to relax and imbibe—perhaps a tad more than he should have. To be fair, he was due a well-deserved drink just to freshen his very dry and dusty throat. However, as we all know, one is never enough when you have a drouth,[46] and unfortunately for John, two were not nearly enough. As Burns put it, he was getting 'fou and unco happy', and John's continued drinking that night in Stirling markedly changed his life. Whilst buying items from a peddler he stole a few others. Sometime later he was arrested and incarcerated in the Tolbooth while awaiting trial. When he was searched he was found to have six folding knives, 24 yellow metal buttons, six bone combs, garter strings, six pairs of stockings, three blue bonnets and four and a half yards of tartan cloth[47]—quite a spree!

The Tolbooth, where John was searched!

When his case was heard a few weeks later, in order to avoid a trial, he freely admitted his wrongdoings and voluntarily banished himself from the Kingdom of Scotland for the rest of his life. The phrase he used was: 'in all time coming during my lifetime'. He was represented in court by a Burgess from Glasgow, who on John's behalf had already organised transportation to His Majesty's Plantations in America. It is thought John was of the opinion that by arranging his own lifelong transportation, he would be spared a worse fate at the hands of the town Magistrates. As far as is known, John did not return to his home in Lochaber and never saw his family again. But maybe that was not the end of the story. Perhaps he did return—or did he arrange for his family to join him in America? Who knows?

Roman Around Stirling

Murray is always keen on the Romans, and we have heard before of their conquest of Scotland and the trade that they conducted with the locals. All those hobnailed sandals marched this way, thousands and thousands of men went north while slaves, grain, cows and timber went south. This exchange was not undertaken on a cash basis, as there were no native coins in Scotland. Agricola's army marched over the Bannock Burn in the AD 80s and kept going north until they hit Elgin, when they probably came back down the Spey, passing Aberdeen. The Roman Army, like any state organisation, is always interested in PR and liked to get people on side. So they frequently gave out gifts – but like any bureaucracy, they can be cack-handed. The gift the Romans passed out in Aberdeen was a wine strainer. Roman wine tended to be a bit pithy and needed sieved. This move was designed to ensure that the locals started buying Roman wine and vessels. Except, of course, this sieve did not work, so was simply a rather useless ornament.

A Truly Dreadful Act

Our final tale concerns an unnamed woman who was taken across the burn against her will soon after the 16th of September 1597 at the command of King James VI.[48] She had been tortured and was facing more torture; she would have been bound and may have been wearing a branks or scold's bridle—and she would soon be executed, for she was condemned as an enemy of the King, State and God: she was an accused witch. James was obsessed with witches; he believed they were real, and thought he had survived an assassination attempt by North Berwick witches. In James' mind witches were agents of the devil, intent on the overthrow of the state and God's anointed king (James had a very big opinion of himself). James had just published his book on witchcraft, *Daemonologie*, and no doubt imagined himself Scotland's leading authority. The unnamed woman had been freshly 'pricked' by the authorities in Stirling and the king

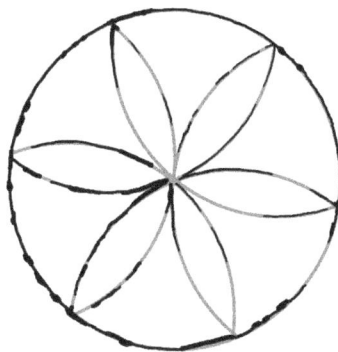

Witch marks from the King's Rooms at Stirling Palace.

was interested in further interrogation. Pricking was a process where a bronze pin was repeatedly driven into an accused witch's body to locate a spot where no pain was felt —as it was believed such a spot was where the devil had touched them to seal their compact. There was, of course, no recognition of the effects of torture, blood loss and sleep deprivation, or that these poor women would have just wanted it all to end, whatever the cost. These were truly despicable crimes and this unfortunate woman was one of around 2,500 people—mostly women—executed for witchcraft in Scotland; crimes of which they were not only innocent but which were impossible to commit.[49]

To lighten the tone on a very dark period of Scottish history, one very peculiar preoccupation of the mostly male investigators, revealed from the trial transcriptions, was about the devil's member (his little Nick, if you will), which is apparently ice cold!

The English Day 1 Camp from the Battle of Bannockburn

To return to the walk, carry on up the hill with your back to the ford. The high ground in front of you is Croftside Farm (280399, 689702, 56° 05' 06" N 3° 55' 25" W) which is where the bulk of the English army camped during Day 1 of the Battle of Bannockburn. But we have perhaps heard enough about that battle, so let's crack on (although we are following the English army's path). Eventually the path comes to a T-junction with a bench (280399, 689702, 56° 05' 06" N 3° 55' 25" W), where Ian and Murray had lunch. All of sudden you will start to see people

The site of the English Camp on Day 1 of Bannockburn.

again, as this is a popular dog-walking and jogging route. There is a hustle and bustle here, creeping in from Bannock Burn itself.

Now, while we didn't go this way, it's well worth standing at the top of the steps that lead down into the Bannock Burn gorge (twice the height of the one we scrambled up). This was what restricted the movement of the English army as it moved to the overnight camp and would present an impressive barrier to any troops fleeing the eventual rout. Can you imagine the English troops? They lost the battle and were now lost, strangers behind enemy lines, hordes of baying Scots hot on their heels, driven into a righteous revenge-driven frenzy, tripping over sharp ripping brambles and dog roses; every aspect of Scotland turning against the invaders.

However, if you do go down that way you will hit what is locally known as the Mill Dam but, yes, you've guessed it—it's a weir with a pond. This is one of the few remaining pieces of evidence of Bannockburn's industrial past.

However, whatever one chooses to call it, one thing is certain: it is a substantial feature on the Bannock Burn, well-known locally as a good fishing spot and in days long gone for swimming and jumping. The main lade that emerged, serviced, among others, a series of now long gone mills including the Skeoch Mill on the outskirts of Bannockburn; a very important place in Scottish history to which we will return. The lade is largely filled in and overgrown today, although with a bit of searching it is just possible to trace its footprint.

East Plean Mining Disaster
As you will have noticed during your earlier experience walking through lime-laden Swallowhaugh, the whole of the burn's course—and indeed Stirling—runs across ancient lime and coal sills. Like the industry surrounding lime extraction, coal mining also played a crucial role in the economy; not just along the Bannock Burn. As indicated earlier, underground geological activity some two to three hundred million years ago created the Stirling Sill, which was dug into and mined for 300–400 years along the lower reaches of the Bannock Burn and in nearby villages.[50] In fact, if it were not for the coal, some of these villages may not exist today. However, there

is little of that infrastructure left to see. If you have been following our routes, the first you would have encountered (and perhaps the nearest to the burn) was Pirnhall Colliery. It was just on the south of Milton and on the south bank of the burn, across the burn from Haughfield where the sulkies raced. The colliery is no more and the site is now the office complex of Ogilvie Homes,[51] built upon the mining waste containing the fossilised remains of the giant ferns that formed the coal so very long ago.

There were some small mines in the general area of Whins of Milton and the area of Bannockburn village, but again little is left to observe. There were also three mine entrances on the right side of the burn, from about the area of Beaton's Mill and beyond Bannockburn village. It is believed the entrances were filled in some years ago. The more

obvious mines in their day were at those at Plean and Fallin; today there is an open air mining museum in Fallin (280399, 689702, 56° 05' 06" N 3° 55' 25" W), to commemorate the Polmaise and the Millhall pits. The most obvious reminder of this former industry awaits us further along our trip where an old mineral railway has been turned to a cycle way, which cuts through toxic bings and railway sidings.

The East Plean explosion mining memorial.

After the bench we kept going up the hill towards the houses. Now, if you do not know this you will miss it, as there is nothing left but street names: we were at the corner of Coal Wynd and Newlands Road (283810, 691517, 56° 06' 08" N 3° 52' 10" W). Coal Wynd was where miners walked to the pits and Newlands was the name of a tiny hamlet, no more than a row that stood at the end of the road, just a minute or two along it. All gone now, but this was where William Robertson Lennie and his wife lived. William died along with twelve of his friends on the 13th of July 1922 in the East Plean Pit, in an explosion a mile underground. There is a very graphic description from one of the survivors, Mr Frank McCann, who was with his son Bernard:

'I... immediately picked up my light and shouted up to the two boys that it was gas. We had only 100 feet to go to reach the level road, but on getting about half way we were knocked down in the dark. We met the whole fumes—just clouds. We had a terrible struggle to get into the level road and after that I could not tell any more. It was an awful explosion. I don't understand why my son Bernard did not escape. I lost him at the foot of the heading... No one has any idea of what it is unless he has come through it.'

Can there be a more poignant example of survivor's guilt? And can you imagine having to return to work, to the thing that took your son and nearly took you?

One final word on mining in the area of the Bannock Burn: the historic miner's strike of 1984 started here, at Polmaise. On February 18th 1984 the miners at Polmaise Colliery, Fallin, downed tools.[52] While their intention was to keep their pit open, as things turned out, they were the first in the fight to keep all the British pits open. The ball was rolling, and shortly afterwards the remainder of the Scottish coalfields joined Polmaise—a serious strike was underway. In March the Yorkshire miners also came out, followed a few weeks later by most of the other English and Welsh coalfields. Nottinghamshire had a partial strike and stayed divided. Whatever

James III's view before his fatal defeat.

way you looked at it, by the end of March 1984 the government had a national coal strike to contend with. There is a certain arrogance in some accounts from the English press who say the strike started in mid-March, omitting to mention that the Scottish coalfields, starting with Polmaise, had already been out some weeks before.[53]

Mustering to Folly

The contrast between the clammy underground pits and the clean open air is never more obvious than on the walk that the miners would've made up Coal Wynd to Coal Hill, which has the best view of Stirling in the city (283810, 691517, 56° 06′ 08″ N 3° 52′ 10″ W). This amazing spot is the scene of James III's final act of folly in a rather lacklustre career.[54] This was where he mustered his troops for the Battle of Sauchieburn, thinking he was emulating his much greater great-great-great-great granddad, Robert the Bruce—even going so far as to carry Bruce's sword into battle. Anyway, James gave up the key strategic advantage provided by the Bannock Burn

Bannockburn at its industrial peak, from the 1930s.

gorge (which is huge at this point) and crossed it to meet his son. To get the best view, you have to climb into the field (look at all those padlocks) and walk past the communication mast (though watch out for the cowpats). The view extends all the way from Earl's Hill to The Forth.

Finally in Bannockburn

So, we went back to the road and then down the other side, into Bannockburn and the absolute delight that is Main Street (280849, 690348, 56° 05′ 28″ N 3° 55′ 00″ W), the core of the town. We went left, but to your right is a fine artisan butchers (great steak pies) and also the Bannockburn Coffee House, if you want a wee break and a tasty treat. So Bannockburn is a lively and independent place, with a proud industrious identity—but it is a shadow of its former self.

In its manufacturing heyday—the mid 1800s and on into the 1900s—Bannockburn was a country village with a population of 2,200 souls containing, amongst other things: three churches, two manses, two schoolhouses, eight public houses, four carpet mills, two cloth mills, one tannery and two substantial stone bridges. The tannery and mills straddled the banks of the Bannock Burn to our left. The majority of the population in these halcyon days was employed locally in the manufacture of cloth and carpets.

The place was so busy that they even built over the burn in a few places. The picture

John Crayton on the banks of the Bannock Burn. Thanks to John and his daughter Jane Hay.

adjacent is of John Crayton, who was 14 in 1952 and is pictured outside his uncle's building right on the banks of the Bannock Burn to the north of Spittal's Bridge. He tells a story of his grandfather, who probably did the first archaeological dig on the Bannockburn Battlefield and claimed to have found decisive evidence of Edward II's troubled retreat along the Bannock Burn. What was this evidence? Two horse shoes stamped E2, supposedly for Edward II! While it's clear that Edward was a show-off (he brought his own poet Robert Baston to battle to document his victory), it's not clear that he went as far as personalised horseshoes!

All of the former hustle and bustle is now gone, but before we head down the hill what about some Bannockburn tales? Our source for the first two tales is the lovely Bennie Tortolano—a man of Italian origin, now in his nineties, who can trace his local history back to the 1890s when his great grandfather emigrated to Scotland from Italy.

The first story relates to the history of Italian emigration to Scotland. It occurred in the late 1890s when many families stuffed all their important belongings into suitcases, gathered up their children and left their homes and life —in this case in the Casino area of Italy—to relocate in the promised land, the United States of America.

A few weeks later, the ship in which they were sailing docked at a port. The purser announced they had arrived in the United States and helped them carry all their worldly possessions onto the quayside. The gangways were raised, and these families stood on their new land: the promised land.

Some of the new settlers, including our informant's great-grandfather's family, headed east from the port, eventually arriving in a quaint 'American' fishing village on the coast, going by the name Fisherrow. The next settlement to the east of the quaint fishing village is the larger metropolis of Musselburgh. It is not recorded when the truth first dawned on them, or how they found out that their promised land was in fact Scotland.

No matter, they were resourceful and found ways to survive, and soon they had a small ice cream café. Despite the success of that venture, his great-grandfather longed for a piece of ground to work and grow his own produce, and when the opportunity to move on again came along, he did. Bannockburn was that opportunity, and became the settled family home.

Bennie's second tale was related with considerable relish. You cannot walk this way and be unaware of the Millhall Ghost. He— because those who have witnessed the ghost are clear that it is male—appears walking behind you, or so those who have cast eyes on him describe it. They say they get a sort of 'someone is watching me, following me' feeling. A quick, nervous look behind and there he is: the Millhall Ghost, walking slowly a few paces behind. Not trying to catch up with those who observe him—just eerily keeping pace. There is no sound, no wailing or other ghostly noises; not even a paranormal smell that other ghostly encounters talk of. No cigar smell, no rotten fruit or even perfume. No, this ghost utters no sound nor emits any odour. Eyewitnesses all say he appears at dusk, in the gloaming, and describe him thus: a tall person with long grey hair, thigh-length boots, with what looks like a long coat or cloak and some kind of headwear that nobody can describe. He is a ghostly, whitish grey. Strangely, something always distracts the observer and when they look back, he is gone.

Portrait of Grand Duke Alexander Pavlovich, The Future Emperor Alexander I of Russia. Image used from *www.heritagemuseum.org*, courtesy of The State Hermitage Museum, St Petersburg, Russia.

Suggestions as to who he may be and why he wanders between Millhall, the Forth and the Bannock Burn vary, and are as mysterious as the actual ghost. Is he a Fallin poacher who drowned a century before and is looking for his loved ones? Others suggest he is the lost soul of an ancient miner. The most interesting came from a person who was sure

she did hear a noise—a horse whinnying—and she was convinced he was a horseman from King Edward's army, searching for his lost horse. We passed the area well before dusk and did not encounter the Millhall Ghost, so we have no view on the subject other than to say: don't look behind you.

Our third and final story is a well-known one in Bannockburn and involves the Russian Tsar. It comes from the pen and the unstinting research of the late Bob McCutcheon, a notable local character and a renowned local historian and scholar, based in his now-gone but still-famous Stirling bookshop. This is the Story of The Tsar's Clock.

During the 18th century, a number of soldiers were passing through St Ninians towards Bannockburn, heading south after the battle of Culloden; it is not said who the soldiers were or what regiment they were from, or if they were even Scottish. In those days, it was not unknown for members of soldier's families to follow them between camps and sometimes to battle zones. While the regiment passed through, the young daughter of one of the soldiers wandered away and became lost. Her name was Betty Willcox. It seems a search of sorts was carried out to locate the child, but to no avail. The soldiers were unable to spend any more time on the search and headed off to wherever they were bound, leaving the young girl to her fate. A local man called Anthony Dunning found the young girl and adopted her.[55] She stayed with him until she was old enough to work and her new father got her work on a farm at Carronbridge.

In 1777 Betty, now a young lady, fell pregnant and gave birth to a son (rumour has it the father was the local laird). When the boy, John Duncan, had grown, he became a sailor on a merchant ship—the *Anne Spittal*, sailing out of Alloa. Fate then intervened, and at some unrecorded point he was press-ganged[56] into the Royal Navy.

In his service, John Duncan found himself in the 1807 to 1812 war with Russia. The majority of that war seems to have been naval, with warships engaging in the Baltic and Barents Seas. He was captured and found himself a prisoner of war in Russia. His mother took it upon herself to make a direct plea to Tsar Alexander I and ask him to release and return her son. By coincidence, Alexander and John were the same age. Betty could not write, so she dictated the following to Alexander Bruce, a local weaver:

Unto the most excellent Alexander Emperor of all the great Dominions of Russia and the territories thereto belonging.

Your most humble servant most humbly begges your Most Gracious Pardon for my boldness in approaching your Most Dread Sovering for clemency at this time.

My Sovering the conclusion; of this Freedom is on account of my son whose name is John Duncan aged 26 years who was Prentiss with Robert Spittle his master Captain of the *Anne Spittle* at that time of the British Embargo in your Sovering's Dominion in Russia and is the only support of me his mother and Beside I have no other freeze for my support to accept this small Present from your Ever Well-wisher while I have breath. The said present is three pairs of Stockens for going on when your Sovering goes a hunting. If your Sovering will be pleased to accept of this and favour me with an answer of this by Bearer and let me know what family of Children Your Sovering has, I will send some stockens for them for the Winter before Winter comes on also what Sons and Dochters you might have.

Most Dread Sovering I am your most obedient Servant till Death.

Elizabeth Willcox[57]

The stockens (socks) were knitted using a special yarn, indigo blue silk, intertwined with white cotton, creating a pattern called 'the sea wave'. Betty had to walk all the way to Paisley to get the yarn—a round trip of about sixty miles.

Her parcel and letter were taken to Russia on a ship sailing from Kincardine on Forth. One of the Tsar's physicians, James Wylie,[58] collected the package and letter and delivered both to Alexander. The letter requesting her son's release and three pair of socks seemed to have moved the Tsar, and he immediately ordered John Duncan's release. In addition, he also paid Betty, via his Ambassador, one hundred pounds (quite a lot of money for three pairs of socks, in any age). Betty used some of the money to have a local clockmaker, David Somerville, make a grandfather clock for her. On a wooden panel under the dial, these words were put:

'Who wad hae thocht it
Stockings wad hae bocht it'

The clock was eventually passed down through John to his son and later to his grandson. He and his wife lived in Smart's

The yarn that made socks fit for a tsar!

Close, Bannockburn and when he died his wife took possession of the clock. No one now knows where the clock is—but if you do, please tell us!

Towards the end of writing this book, contact was made with a woman in Perthshire—a distant relative of the Willcox family—who has in her possession remnants of the yarn Betty used to knit the 'stockens' for the Tsar. We were lucky enough not only to see the yarn remnant, but to get a photograph of it.

Victorian poet Hugh Scott Riddell, while staying in Bridge of Allan, complains of one of Somerville's clocks, which seems very reminiscent of our recent Covid-19 lockdown: 'Confined by rain to the house. Tormented by a clock, the most solemn, precise, pedantic horologe that ever proclaimed the flight of time. It has just struck eleven, and in the same space of time might with moderate rapidity have struck thirty. How it will manage to get through its meridian task, I wot not. It is animated, I verily believe, by the ghost of a dominie (Scots for teacher). There is a certain nasal twang of most insufferable conceit in every stroke. Twang (long pause) Twang Twang—a most villainous highland tone, and yet, on inspection, I find the clock was made by D. Somerveil of St Ninians. It rains profusely, but tho' it should pour like the Forth, I will fly from this house when warning is given of St Ninians' noonday operations. I could not endure to hear the snivelling, drawling block head twanging one dozen mortal blows on the empty skull of the patient bell. I wish I could commit to paper the image in my mind's eye of the old snuffy dominie with his scratch wig of penurious locks, and long-backed, broad-skirted blue coat, but I am not a Harvey or a Macduff or a Wilkie else I should exorcise that clock and make its professor the pedagogue stand forth in black and white. After 12 I shall have peace for 4 or 5 hours, but then my trials will begin again anew. How the evening is to be got thus I cannot tell. Hark is that the warning of Ringan let me fly.'

Spittals and Spitals: A Field Guide
At the bottom of the hill is the likely location of first a ford, and latterly Robert Spittal's 16th century bridge. Now, Robert Spittal (or Spettal or Spitall) was James IV's tailor, and on his death he left money for bridges[59] across

The splendid Spittal Bridge.

Peace 1710. 12 feet added to the breadth by the trustees 1781'.

This bridge has had a complex history. Looking under it are clearly two phases, and there is a record of another repair in 1631—is it still a 16th century bridge? It's a bit like Murray's dad's hammer, which he assured his son belonged to the famous Chippendale[61]—expanding that while he had to change the shaft three times over the years, the head had only been replaced once.

Now, we said that there was a originally a ford here, and we know this because Murray once helped to make a TV programme here called *River Hunters*, which involved metal detection of key locations on river and stream beds. The pitch was great: the director, a lovely chap from the deep south of England, assured me that this was going to resolve the Battle of Bannockburn. Murray remarked that we knew what happened as well as more or less where—this did not go down well.

Stirling and for a charity or almshouse, which was called Spittal's Hospital or 'Spittal's Spital'! Spital, with one 't', is a medieval contraction of hospital, which is more to do with religious hospitality than an A&E. Stirling, with its rich medieval history, is full of spitals, including at least one Knights Templar institution. Robert Spittal's family is probably from a farm owned or established by one of the hospitals, hence his name. On the side of Spittal's bridge it says:

'This bridge was built by Robert Spitall taylor to King James the Fourth 1516 pro patria et posteris.[60] Repaired by the Justices of the

The written accounts do talk of bodies lying thick at the conclusion of the battle, so it seemed a reasonable strategy to target the burn. So off we went and we encountered some amount of rubbish, cans, fish knives, car batteries and road signs. But amongst the dross was something which did not make the final cut: a tiny 2cm piece of genuine treasure in the form of a Roman period dragonesque fibula. A divine object, but so corroded as to be impossible to photograph. Fibulas are wee brooches, so this was lost here nearly 2,000 years ago as someone crossed the burn. Did they fall? Were they in a hurry? Did they hear the splash and then panic? Where did they get it? Was it a gift from a lover? We shall never know, but these mysteries are why Murray is an archaeologist.

The Birth of Tartan

While this place is currently a pleasant green valley, as we've heard, one hundred years ago it was full of mills, the associated processing activity leaving the burn full of industrial waste. However, this place is also the modern birthplace of one of the world's most recognisable brands: tartan![62] Now just to be clear, I'm not talking about kilts: there's no way we're going near that hornet's nest—though kilts really are ancient and are definitely not an English invention, whatever you might read online. Tartan and gridded woven cloth is also ancient, and has been found all over the world, but is most frequently associated with Scotland.[63]

Earlier on, we heard of a very important place in Scottish history at the heart of Bannockburn: the Skeoch mill, which was situated on the south bank of the Bannock Burn (although it eventually extended across the burn), next to Spittal's Bridge. It was built circa 1770 by William Wilson to make carpets and tartan. This mill succeeded a series of individual single-room houses, each with their own loom. The mill developed from a typical medium-sized family-run mill into a compact industrial complex with spinning-mills, weaving sheds and dye-houses, as well as workers' housing. It became so successful that the Bannock Burn itself was eventually built over. A crucial part of textile manufacturing, particularly involving wool, involves cleansing the raw material, cloth or wool to remove impurities, such as oils, dirt and other contaminates. That process is called *fulling* or, in Scots, *wauking*. It is carried out in two parts: scouring and milling. Part of that process involves beating the material with a club, or by the use of feet and/or hands. Gaels in Scotland would sing traditional wauking songs in rhythm to the pace of the beating. As water mills developed through medieval times, the process was mechanised and the traditional process mostly died out. One has to assume that somewhere in the mill complex, a building for wauking would be present and perhaps rhythmical singing could be heard.

So successful was this business that by the 1860s, half the population of Bannockburn lived in houses owned by the Wilsons—and the annual value of production was around £80,000, which is probably around £9,000,000 in today's money. But how exactly did all that happen? Well, following the Jacobite Rising of 1745–46, the British Government banned the wearing of tartan. Now just think through that: a piece of clothing was considered so dangerous that it was banned. Was the British state really so fragile that tartan threatened it? Well, apparently it was, and this is where the Disarming Act of 1746 comes in. However, the whole thing is far more complex; it was Highland Clothing that was banned and not tartan, and the act applied to men and boys not women and girls, exempted British Army soldiers or members of the gentry. So there was still lots of tartan being worn. Ultimately it was attempt to ban a particular type of clothing associated with the Jacobites, but it was hard to enforce and often ignored.

The ban only affected 'that part of North Britain called Scotland', as defined in an earlier Act that followed the 1715 Rising. In reality, it only applied north of a line from Dumbarton to Perth. Now, while the ban was lifted in 1782, the story goes that our canny hero William realised that Stirling was south of the Highland Line, so he could steal a march on his competitors. He and his family made a fortune selling tartan to expats across the Empire, and eventually gaining a contract for the military. It's not entirely clear how the variety and flexibility of regional patterns became associated with particular clans, and there is a suspicion that the Wilsons may have helped create these associations in order to boost sales.

The birth of Tartan... the date stone from probably the world's first Tartan factory!

Given that tartan was never really banned, what does this actually mean? Perhaps it was just added to the family's history to explain their success, or perhaps in the 18th century there really was a widespread reticence to manufacture tartan north of the Highland Line? Regardless, the Wilsons of Bannockburn stand at the start of a global brand and industry. The only physical survivor of the Skeoch Mill is a date stone currently stored in the grounds of the Smith Museum and Art Gallery.

The 19th century saw a tartan craze as Queen Victoria popularised it, but it all kicked off when Walter Scott presented George IV with full Stuart tartan garb in 1822, despite having at one time dismissed the whole idea of clan tartans as a 'fashion of modern date'. This was the first visit of a reigning British monarch to Scotland since the 17th century,[64] so it was a really major event and it really put Scotland and its romanticised past (as composed by Scott) on the international map. The monarch arrived in Leith on his yacht, the *Royal George*, and welcomed Sir Walter Scott aboard with the greeting: 'Sir Walter Scott, the man in Scotland I most want to see'. The King called for wine and drank to his health, after which the Monarch peregrinated through Edinburgh to tumultuous acclaim, bedecked in Stuart tartan, sporting a feather and thistle on his bonnet. It was Scott who organised the Royal visit—again playing a role in putting tartan back into the public conscience, whether by design or not, and whether he believed tartan to be a fashion of modern date or not.

The Wilsons ended up owning the wonderful Bannockburn House, which is now run by volunteers and well worth a visit. However, over time they faced ever-fiercer competition; the mills closed, and eventually were all demolished by Stirling Council.

The only two mill buildings still standing in Bannockburn are, firstly, an old carpet factory situated on the north side of the burn, adjacent to the wide pathway at that point and roughly two hundred yards west of Spittal's Bridge. The other is the Royal George next to Telford's Bridge; also an old carpet factory, and originally driven by its own weir (look for the wheel pit on the left side of the building). Some say the mill is named after the King's Royal Yacht, the *Royal George*, and certainly it was opened the same year as the royal visit! Certainly, the visit was important enough for the aforementioned date stone from Skeoch Mill to have been

The arch of the water wheel at The Royal George Mill.

reinscribed in 1822. The Royal George mill is now home to The Bruce and Thistle 312 Masonic Lodge.

Andrew Templeton's Love
We hope you will forgive a wee aside from an unjustly forgotten poet, Andrew Templeton, who walked here before it was grass. He worked for the Wilsons before setting up as a general merchant in the village. He was simply known as 'the poet', and was by all accounts a very nice and caring chap. One of his best is called 'The Husband's Song', and is a beautiful ode to a life- long love:

Our love is no the wild romance
That youthfu' dreamers cherish, O;
Nor like the lighting's hasty glance,
That brightens but to perish, O.
'Tis like the fountain rising pure,
Or like a flowing river, O;

Telford's wonderful bridge.

Our mutual love shall aye endure,
And grow and bloom for ever, O.

Now we think this recalls the best of John Donne's 'A Valediction Forbidding Mourning' which, if you don't know it, is well worth reading if you have ever loved someone and been parted from them. Beautiful!

Telford's New Bridge

Now immediately to the right on the Royal George Mill is the magnificent Telford Bridge, built and designed by one of Scotland's greatest engineers. He was born in 1757 and hailed from Langholm in the Scottish Borders where, like the famous author James Hogg, was due to become a shepherd. While the bridge and the mill seem to have been designed as one, the bridge is slightly older and dates from 1819. There was some thought given to celebrating its birthday, but no one is quite sure when it was formally opened. The bridge spans the burn like a giant H.G. Wells creature and has a very unusual, if not unique, character in that the design of the curved masonry struts was Telford's brilliant solution to reducing lateral inward earth-pressure movement of the tall abutments. Unusual, perhaps, but nevertheless effective. It is best viewed from the public park to the east.

Balquidderock Wood

We find the best way is to walk up the west slope, along the path from Ladywell Park and walk towards Bannockburn High School's playing field (280849, 690348, 56° 05′ 28″ N 3°

The probable route through Balquidderock that Bruce took on Day 2 of The Battle of Bannockburn.

55′ 00″ W). You are now following the route taken by the Scots' on the morning of Day 2 of The Battle of Bannockburn. Follow the path through the wood, down to the 10,000 year old raised beach and towards the bed of a lost sea, where whales once swam.[65] During the last Ice Age, the weight of the glaciers that covered the land at the time pushed Scotland down, completely depressing the whole nation (a bit like the football results). As the ice retreated, Scotland began to slowly rise up again—a process called isostatic bounce— and the water began to drain out, gradually turning the area into a bog.

The wood's name is Gaelic and is named for a now-lost farm, the name literally meaning 'the farm with plentiful straw', i.e. a fertile plot. It's full of gnarled, twisted, ancient oaks, a mini-Fangorn Forest, though there are no Ents to be seen. This is one of those spine-tingling spots, and we really mean it. This is where the Scots army stopped, looked at the English camp below and prayed before entering the fray. This story is much better appreciated from the site of the English camp, so we will pick it up again when we get there.

At the bottom of the wood, turn right and walk to the south of the new housing (called Caltrop Place, named to commemorate the battlefield). Right in the middle of the woods, just to your right, is a big isolated wall (280849, 690348, 56° 05′ 28″ N 3° 55′ 00″ W), completely incongruous. You can climb and have a look if you want (Murray did), but there's nothing to see—the big wall just sits there, mute and silent. This is the backstop for the targets of the local rifle club, which operated in the late 19th and early 20th centuries; a time when people were encouraged to train with guns so that they might serve in the military for the good of the Empire.

* * *

Endnotes

28) The current Chartershall House, which is now private, was built as a convalescence home for 16 patients recovering from illness which opened in 1906.

29) We know the name of one possible nail-maker here or nearby. Prior to the sixth of February 1859, John Gow was happily engaged as a nailer at Chartershall. On that date he left nail making to take up the role as police officer at Glasgow water works.

30) One of them may have been a sewing teacher.

31) To my brothers' eternal shame, when children they would occasionally pop into a local shop and ask the shopkeeper, who was bald, if they could borrow his comb. Both are now sober, respectable citizens.

32) The Hawkie life size statue features in the William Gemmell collection in Eaglesham and was carved from life. William was a joiner and untrained artist who, as a hobby, constructed several life-size statues, and his statues are well worth a visit. Some are so heavy that they had to be stored on the ground floor.

33) Don't believe that guff about the siege and midsummer!

34) For those lacking familiarity with Scots, a square go is a one-on-one fight, which tends to take place in Glasgow on Saturday nights.

35) The aforementioned nail-making industry led to the creation of a series of fake battle axes and caltrops, all of which were regularly 'discovered' and available for sale to gullible visitors. These days of course while no one will offer you a fake, they will instead try to sell you any amount of tartan tat or Bruce fridge magnets.

36) The crow wood. Now you will sometimes see it written as Corbiewood, but we spoke to people who raced there and they call it Corbie Wood... so that's what we've done too.

37) On top of the Stirling Bridge battlefield, where Wallace met his destiny.

38) In later years it also featured greyhound racing.

39) Surprisingly, many Standardbred horses return back to the USA and retire to a new life amongst the Amish, as carriage or driving horses... and may even have made it into Harrison Ford's film *Witness*?

40) Originally from just up the road in Kippen.

41) Probably a relative of the more famous Citizen Jaffray, who around 1800 inoculated several thousand people against smallpox and helped free a slave.

42) For those that want to read more on the nail trade we recommend: John G Harrison's *Notes on the History of the Nail Trade in Scotland 1500–1800*, July 2013, and the book, *Carron: Where the Iron Flows Like Water* by Brian Watters.

43) We have figures for the trade from around 1600 forward, and this is likely to be a gross underestimate. That is an awful lot of dung. Indeed, an 1812 tourist guide to Stirling, basically the first ever written, concludes by saying that the author was pleased to report that in 1811 the Magistrates of Stirling had sold the town dung for a sum nearly equal to that which they had spent clearing it two years prior. The precise cubic tonnage involved, and what it cost, is at no point made clear. The present authors are even more delighted to reassure any prospective visitors to our fair city that the town is now completely free from large dung heaps! Those wishing to find ordure should direct their attention to Westminster where it is produced in abundance.

44) The Battle of Sauchieburn was designated by Historic Environment Scotland as of National Significance in their Inventory of Battlefields.

45) A corbel is a structural feature jutting from building to support a weight.

46) The very thirsty state most Scotsmen find themselves after the completion of an onerous task.

47) Which as we shall learn may have come from further up the burn for Bannock Burn is the home of tartan.

48) We can be so precise because the associated letter is in the Stirling Council Archives.

49) We recommend that anyone interested in this topic spend some time with the Scottish Witchcraft Survey, which can be found online via the University of Edinburgh's School of History, Classics and Archaeology.

50) In the medieval period the Royal Court at Stirling sourced coal from Royal Lands at Skeoch (not the mill further up the burn), which are first recorded in a Charter of Robert The Bruce's.

51) Who helped recover the North Third Spitfire.

52) These miners had a proud tradition of doing what was right. After WW2, when houses were in short supply, 10 children aged between 1–15 slept on straw over a concrete floor in an air raid shelter at Bandeath. Others were turned away by Polish soldiers based there, and four adults and 10 children walked until 4am to simply keep warm. The resulting evictions and prosecutions led to 400 men to strike at the Plean pits in protest.

53) It is difficult to separate the mining industry from its use of child labour in the past. In the 18th century, a quarter of the workforce were children. As late as 1842, 12 year old John Allan had worked the pits at Plean—from the age of 10, he worked

12–13 hours a day, struggling through flooded tunnels which reached over his knees.

54) His main achievement was to marry Margaret, the daughter of the King of Denmark, and gain the Orkney and Shetland Isles as part of the dowry.

55) If this seems unlikely, in 1747 Stirling Burgh accounts record payments made to look after two children left behind by soldiers.

56) Kidnapped to serve in the military. These gangs were notorious in Stirling, where soldiers regularly descended from the Castle. In May 1702 one Captain Sharp pointed a loaded gun at Patrick McFarland to take him back to the Castle, but a woman named Mareon McFarlane grabbed the gun and said he would 'shoot none at that time'. This incident became known as the Women's Riot— bravo!

57) The letter, or perhaps the story of its contents, was preserved in the family.

58) Or to give him his full title: Sir James Wylie, 1st Baronet, President of the Imperial Medical and Surgical Academy, who was from Tulliallen just along the road but is buried in St Petersburg.

59) His most famous bridge is across the Teith at Doune, which he apparently funded after a dispute with a ferryman! He also funded the Auld Brig over the Devon at Tullibody. In 1560, the latter was damaged by William Kirkcaldy of Grange to impede the progress of French soldiers heading from Leith to Stirling Castle. They were in Scotland at the behest of Marie of Guise, mother of Mary Queen of Scots. The French commander that day, Henri

Cleutin, repaired the gap in the bridge by using parts of the roof of Tullibody Kirk.

60) Roughly 'for country and posterity'.

61) The 18th century furniture maker.

62) It is said that Neil Armstrong took a swatch of Armstrong tartan to the moon.

63) What may be the oldest tartan in the world was uncovered in 1933, during excavation work in the Callendar Riggs area of Falkirk. An urn containing the largest-ever hoard of Roman coins in Scotland (payments to keep peace on the Northern Frontier) was discovered with a scrap of yellow and brown cloth, cross woven—tartan! This pattern became the inspiration for the modern Falkirk Tartan.

64) Now the authors, as you may have gathered, are cynical souls and do wonder about this visit being so close to the Radical Rising of 1820, when there were armed revolts across Scotland.

65) The Smith Museum and Art Gallery has some of their bones on display.

STAGE 4
CALTROP PLACE TO THE FORTH

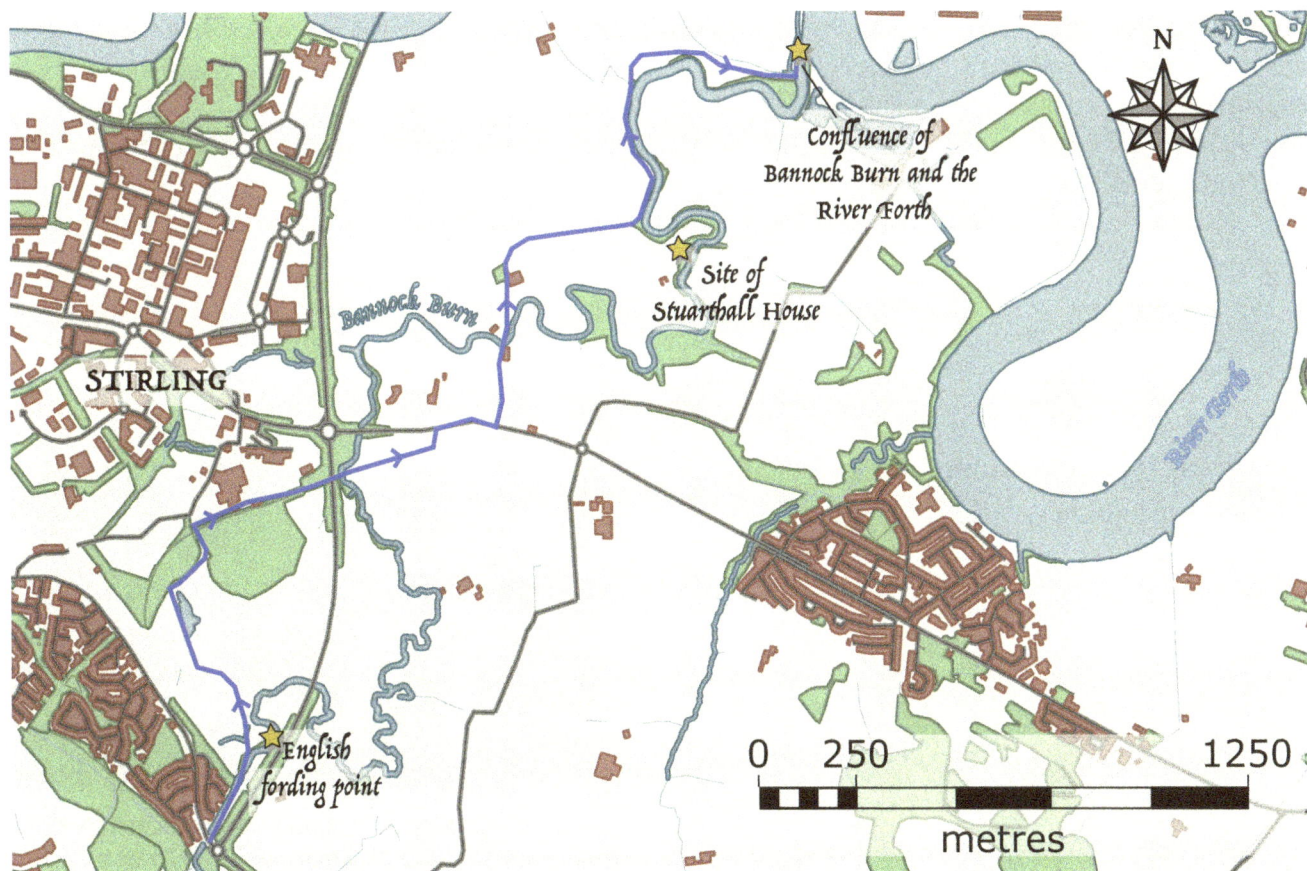

STIRLING

Bannock Burn

Confluence of
Bannock Burn and the
River Forth

Site of
Stuarthall House

River Forth

English
fording point

N

0   250   1250

metres

The Direct Route: 6.4 miles (10.23km)

As the burn begins to meander a lot in this section, the walk is considerably longer than in previous sections, so you can of course simply take the path of least resistance and follow formal tracks and roads. This section is also longer as it includes a return to the road from the burn's confluence with the Forth. This is the route we recommend but not the one we took (we really followed the burn and it was very hard work). After the Caltrop Place houses, cross the road (*281165, 691009, 56° 05' 49" N 3° 54' 43" W*) and then cross under the Thunder Bridge (the railway) and follow the path to the right. This takes you in a western arc round the bing to your right, turn right at the bing (*281123, 692015, 56° 06' 22" N 3° 54' 47" W*) and head east, back towards busy road, following the pathway on the old mineral railway line. Cross through the tunnel and then turn left at the first junction (*281873, 692273, 56° 06' 31" N 3° 54' 04" W*). Head north towards the road (A905) and then turn right and walk along it, crossing into the Stuarthall Farm road (just to the east of the Caravan Park (*282145, 692371, 56° 06' 34" N 3° 53' 48" W)*). Follow the road past Stuarthall Farm and head north along the west bank of the burn (*282632, 693025, 56° 06' 56" N 3° 53' 21" W*) just before Stuarthall itself, after this point it's all fields and fences. Follow the burn on its western bank until you hit the Forth – then return.

How We Did It

So, we decided as were doing this on your behalf that we would do it the hard way and actually follow the burn. This was the first time we had taken this route, and we imagine that we may have been the first people to have ever walked this route since the construction of the new relief road.

The Thunder Bridge

From the east end of Caltrop Place, climb the steps and cross the road (281165, 691009, 56° 05' 49" N 3° 54' 43" W), then go under the railway—which is known as the Thunder Bridge due to the noise from the train (stop

The Thunder Bridge and the ford used by the English troops.

and listen). How many trains a day have passed here since the route was opened in 1848? How many lives, how many stories, lost loves, broken promises, business proposals and, perhaps most poignant, of all the thousands of soldiers heading off to the front? In the 19th century, before the Forth Rail Bridge, Stirling was a central point and soldiers came and went. In World War I, Stirling's population doubled as soldiers were billeted everywhere, including Kings Park. Amongst the thousands of soldiers were territorials from the 1/7th (Leith Battalion), The Royal Scots, heading for Gallipoli in Turkey (the campaign that forged the Anzacs). They had been training in Stirling and transferred to Larbert, where they caught the train to Liverpool. This train was then involved in Britain's worst ever rail crash on 22nd May 1915 at Quintinshill. Some 231 people were killed (214 soldiers, nine passengers, three railway employees and four victims, thought to be children, whose remains were never claimed or identified—which seems incredible). The soldiers were buried in a mass grave in Leith's Rosebank Cemetery, where Murray's parents are buried, so he knows it well.

Bannockburn: Day 2
On the other side of the railway is a pleasant and flat green pasture. Beyond the Bannockburn's gorge, our host opens up and stretches after being cramped and confined, beginning to curve and twist. This is the likely spot of the ford (281358, 691307, 56° 05′ 59″ N 3° 54′ 32″ W) to the English camp and is the core of the most important battle in Scottish history. Without this battle there would be no Scotland – we would simply have become part of England, a province, a rump of a place, another stepping stone to England's greater glory, or as Burns put it:

Fareweel to a' our Scottish fame,
Fareweel our ancient glory;
Fareweel ev'n to the Scottish name,
Sae fam'd in martial story.
Now Sark rins over Solway sands,
An' Tweed rins to the ocean,
To mark where England's province stands.[66]

When you think of Bannockburn and all that it means—all those statues of Robert the Bruce; The Corries and *Flower of Scotland*; Burn's *Scots wa Hae*—you are really thinking of Day 2. As we have heard, Day 1 was just another wee stumble, the English controlled the Castle and most of the army had a day in the sunshine. Yeah, that renegade Bruce had won yesterday, but the English had burnt his baggage train at Cambuskenneth overnight. Today would confirm that Edward II was his father's son, fit to be king. If the Scots did not scatter like mice, he would crush them and celebrate in style at Stirling Castle this evening. God would smile on him and confirm his destiny.

By contrast, Bruce had spent the night planning, seeking council and listening to the reports of his spies. Where was the camp? Was the ground hard or soft? What was their morale like? We wonder if he slept. There was no coffee to keep him awake; just adrenaline and pain. Bruce took the decision to attack, and they marched from Coxet Hill in the dark to arrive in the morning in Balquidderock Wood, where they paused. Abbot Maurice of Inachaffrey stepped ahead and led the Scots in Mass and prayer. Seeing the arrival of the Scots, the well-rested Edward II— perhaps a little groggy from a night of wine and song—asked if the Scots were praying for his mercy. No, the reply came, they were praying for their sins. Remember, Bruce had been excommunicated, so to him this would be trial by combat to demonstrate God's judgment on both the Scots and the English.

At this point it's worth remembering poor old Wallace and his static schiltron. The Scots lost at Falkirk because they could not move and were overwhelmed by the English forces and decimated by the archers. Bruce's tactics on Day 1 were to prepare the ground to ensure

The core of Day 2 of The Battle of Bannockburn, looking to the bing.

that the English could not surround the Scots. How could he achieve the same result on Day 2?

Two key factors will have influenced Bruce's decision. First, the reports of the spies. The English camp lay between the valleys of the Bannock Burn and Pelstream (meaning pool stream), which created a 'V' shape with Balquidderock Wood at the open end of the 'V'. Now, these were not the deep gorges of the burn which we have just walked through. Rather, these were muddy sinuous hollows, which are actually very tricky to cross (as you will learn), especially in armour. The second factor was Bruce's revolutionary change to Scottish tactics—he created mobile schiltrons in which the troops could move in concert with each other. In effect, they could march in formation. Now this might not sound like a big deal to you, but if an army cannot move in order and maintain its discipline, it is just a bunch of people who can be picked off one at a time.

So in principle, these two factors would create the grounds for Bruce's gamble: if the Scots attacked they had the opportunity to push the English into the bottom of the 'V', restricting their movement and thus their ability to flank the Scots. Now, we know what happened—the Scots pushed the English cork back into the bottle of the Pelstream and Bannock Burn's confluence. However, that would merely be a victory. Why did it become a rout, and why did Bannockburn become so rightly famous?

The answer comes back to Bruce's innovation of the mobile schiltron. To march in concert with thousands of others requires lots and lots of training and those who were not trained posed a threat to the whole, like an infected cut. They could not be allowed to take part and were benched. Traditionally, these people were called the Sma' Folk: commoners who fixed the weapons, washed the clothes, baked the bread—but they also included prostitutes, the old, the sick and the young. Bruce was ruthless, so these people had to be excluded. The main account suggests there were around 20,000 of them, and 15,000 descended on the battlefield. Of course, famously, we Scots were and are a free people, keen to play our part and have our fair share, no matter what the King had to say.[67] So, seeing how well the battle was going for the Scots, the Sma' Folk moved from Coxet Hill to the English camp.

The medieval account of Edward II's life, written in the 1320s, describes this onslaught: 'not one of [the Scots] was on horseback, but each was furnished with light armour,[68] which a sword could not easily penetrate. They had axes at their sides and carried lances in their hands. They advanced like a dense hedge, and such a crowd could not easily be penetrated'. This took place where we are now standing.

Now, from the English perspective they were simply losing. Which no doubt came as a big surprise. It really shouldn't be happening, how could a bunch of hairy-arsed Scotch peasants be winning? They were the cream of England, the best in the world: defeat was simply unimaginable. However, all was not lost. Edward II simply had to retreat in good order to the west and to Stirling Castle, which they still controlled. So the orders went out to retreat in good order; the Pelstream was to be boarded so that the army could safely retreat across it and reform for the short hop, skip and jump to the Castle. But... remember the Sma' Folk. Their route from Coxet Hill to the camp took them towards the English line of retreat. From the English point of view, the incoming throngs looked like a fresh Scots army. Can you picture Edward's face as the report of fresh troops reached him? Where did they come from, and how had his own spies let him down so badly? Who could he now trust, and had God deserted him? His army disintegrated, false smiles disappeared and backs were turned as individuals plotted their own escape. As discipline collapsed, the Scots' main force picked people off one by one, with aristocratic leaders captured for ransom and bodies picked over. The result was an overwhelming, crushing Scottish victory—God was on Bruce's side.

We make no apology for going on at such lengths about the Battle of Bannockburn—it's a brilliant story, and must be amongst the greatest military achievements in British history. An aggressive invader was not just beaten back, but utterly smashed with an enormous loss of face and treasure. The poet Robert Baston—who, as we heard, had been taken by the English to Bannockburn to record Edward's 'impending' great victory—instead wrote:

Why do I sing of massacre?... I lack the skill to name the fallen, nor count their numbers, not how they fell, and not how much death they inflicted. Many fell, many were pierced with arrows, many sunk down into the mud and many were captured alive and bound to be ransomed... Across the entire battlefield the space is piled high with plunder and riches.

This was on our minds on as we walked along the burn. The mound to the left, right in the middle of the battlefield, is a bing from mining waste. This came from the Polmaise 1 and 2 shafts, which in 1948 employed 714 people who produced 160,000 tons of coal per annum. The spill from the bing overlies what was Stirling's first swimming pool, which was constructed at the end of the 19th century for miners. It was open air and presumably very bracing. Murray helped organise a small excavation with local children to try to find it, but there was too much rubbish over the top.

The burn represents quite a barrier, and increasingly the land here is dominated by the invasive Himalayan Balsam, making it a bit of struggle to follow. To our right was the massive embankment of Stirling's relief road.

When we hit the relief road bridge over the burn, we walked under it but could not cross the burn itself as it was too deep. While it has meandered, it also here scours itself ever deeper into the carse clay. So we had to climb the bank up to the road, walk along the verge and then down the other side, much to the surprise of people driving along the road—we do not recommend doing this!

The next field, still in the core of the battlefield and just a very typical Scottish field, there are odd, shallow hollows and gullies from relict burns, sometimes lined with hawthorns but most of them are even-sloping gentle things. At the time of the battle, these were all bodies of water, with steeper banks. In the year of the battle there was more rainfall than today, so the water table would be higher. This means that they were considerably harder to cross and acted as traps in the aftermath of the battle, catching fleeing English troops. Certainly all the metal detection finds from the battle, which was conducted by Professor Tony Pollard and GUARD Archaeology for the BBC's programme, are focused here.[69] It's also worth noting that many accounts of the battle stress that as many soldiers drowned as were killed in battle. In effect, we were walking across a mass grave.

The mineral railway provided by Mr Dufton.

Now, Bannockburn was not the end of the Wars of Independence, which ran to 1328—and one of the things we never talk about is the impact of the battle on the people of Stirling. The day after the victory, the Castle surrendered to Bruce and he pulled it down so that it could not be used against him—an act which had a massive impact on the local people. It's also worth noting that there had been an English garrison in Stirling Castle for ten years, and which in 1312 numbered 120 people. The burials of some of this garrison were recovered from the Castle and, if you visit, you can see a facial reconstruction of a very battle-scarred English knight. People are people, so over those ten years not everyone was plotting to undermine English rule. Men and women had to live; they weren't quislings, they were just people. Trade continued, friendships were made, children were born. But in an all-out war, could Bruce ever trust Stirling again? Certainly even if he didn't, he could always rely on the Forth, so he never rebuilt Stirling Castle—though he did invest in Clackmannan to the north of the Forth. All of this, combined with the battle and Bruce's scorched earth policy, had a massive impact on the local economy, which collapsed and was reduced by roughly 55%.[70]

Eventually the burn curves back round to the road and hits the aforementioned former mineral railway to Fallin (281623, 692199, 56° 06′ 28″ N 3° 54′ 18″ W), which is now a cycle way.[71] Under our feet are miles of former mine shafts, all of which once linked Polmaise 1 and 2 to mines 3 and 4 in Fallin, to our east.[72] We went under the motorway to the livestock market, which has a friendly wee café selling teas, coffees, tasty pies and the like (281295, 692190, 56° 06′ 28″ N 3° 54′ 37″ W).

The Most Important Crook in Scotland[73]
After refuelling, we cracked on for the final stretch. The burn is simply too deep and densely wooded to walk its banks here, so we followed the path of the former railway till we hit the first road, then turned left and walked to the road. We then turned left again and walked along the verge to Crook (281716, 692364, 56° 06′ 34″ N 3° 54′ 13″ W), which in the

The confluence of the Bannock Burn and the Pelstream.

18th century was known as Ingram's Crook. Sorry to all the fans of Tartan Noir, but in Scots 'crook' means—amongst many other things—a bend in a river, and is probably a reference to the confluence of the Bannock Burn and the Pelstream, the corner of the English camp. So, of course, we had to go and see that! The burn here is slow and flat, not much of barrier, and straddled between roads. Its setting is gone, and we struggled to imagine the battle.

The little cottage here, which seems to be the last mill on the Bannock Burn, was once home to Elizabeth Hamilton, who lived here with her aunt at the end of the 18th century, her parents having died in her infancy. It was a bit chilly when we got here, and a few lines of her poem 'My Ain Fireside' sprang to our minds:

I ha'e seen great anes, and sat in great ha's,
'Mang lords and fine ladies a' covered wi'
braws;
At feasts made for princes, wi' princes I've
been,
Whare the grand sheen o'splendour has
dazzled my een;
But a sight sae delightfu', I trow, I ne'er spied,
As the bonnie blythe blink o'my ain fireside;
My ain fireside, my ain fireside,
My ain fireside, my ain fireside,
O there's nought to compare wi' ane's ain
fireside.

We could see her very clearly, poking the fire, all toasty and warm while we tramped to the end of our walk!

A loup o' The Forth is worth an Earldom o' The North
This wee couplet, which is first recorded in the Medieval Register of Cambuskenneth Abbey, reveals just how wealthy the land around Stirling could be. However, looking towards the Forth on that final cold damp stretch of the walk, we weren't convinced.

We walked along the northern bank of the Bannock Burn till we hit the road again. All this was rather rough going. The walk from the confluence with the Forth is across a wide arable plain, and to fully understand this landscape we needed to hit the maps.[74] In the middle of the 18th century the area was covered with small farms, some with Gaelic names (like Wester Polmaise—now Stuarthall—which is Gaelic for 'beautiful water'), indicating medieval origins. To the west, closer to Fallin, are the remains of Wester Moss, which was systematically cleared from the 18th century and contains the first recorded mention of Moss Lairds. This is a contemporary 18th century derogatory term for people who cleared the peat from the various bogs and mosses around Stirling and turned it into farmland, often carving igloo-style houses out of the peat. It is often claimed that the bulk of these people were Gaelic-speaking refugees who had been dispossessed after the Jacobite Rising of '45, who found work on George

The late 18th century lime kiln used to transform the carse.

Drummond's Blair Drummond Estate in late 18th century. Except, of course, the Fallin chaps were there nearly forty years earlier.

Around 1750 there were 20 or so small farms across this landscape, but today there are only two or three. The bulk of these farms vanished around 1800, during the period of the Improvements—which we've heard about before. In essence, smaller 'inefficient' farms were replaced with bigger open fields. These Lowland Clearances are far less well known than the later Highland Clearances, and most of the so-called Cottars ended up in the cities, supplying labour for the Industrial Revolution. The clearing of smaller sub-tenants was combined with the stripping of the peat to increase the amount of arable land. However, the resultant land was too acidic and so had to have lime added to it to improve its fertility. This was done here too, with a bespoke late 18th century lime kiln built on the shores of the Forth so that the raw, unburnt limestone could be supplied by boat. As we have heard, the impact of these changes led to a 300% increase in agricultural output, and people came to Scotland from across the world to learn how we'd achieved so much.

The Last Bridge, and Not Nearly Too Far!
As the last bridge on the Bannock Burn appeared, we stopped for a rest. The bridge is not on any of the older maps, and seems to be 19th century in origin. To one—somewhat depressing—side, a collection of Irn Bru cans can be seen, as if someone was regularly finishing them at this point and chucking them from the window. Sometimes people really are scummy.

On the bridge was a mysterious mark: an arrow with a dot at the top. Another mason

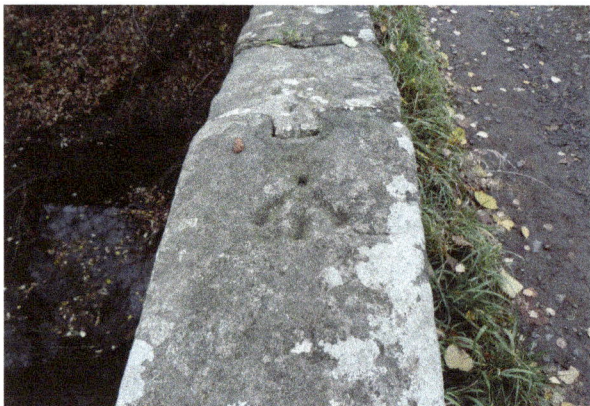

A secret mason's mark?

mark? Murray knew the answer, but Ian was puzzled and as we were chatting, the man that lived in the nearby farmhouse came for a chat. We're not sure he saw many people. He told us about how often his house got flooded, and how tricky the burn was to deal with. And of course, how the flooding could trap him with no way out. Before we crack on, we will tell you that the mark is probably an Ordnance Survey temporary bench mark on a fixed point that they could come back to—all very mundane.

A Desperate Jacobite Plot
The fields were very muddy, so we decided to stick to the road. The very final house on the Bannock Burn is called Steuarthall (which, as we said, was originally Wester Polmaise but renamed in 1784 after James Stewart bought it and named it after himself).[75] Though the current Steuarthall is not actually Wester Polmaise—it's merely the late 18th or early 19th century stable block—it does contain a dated 16th century fireback, obviously from the original house. The house was in the burn's meander to the north of the current Steuarthall. Now, just pause and think: this is really an incredibly remote and defensive location, located in a meander of the burn and surrounded by water on three

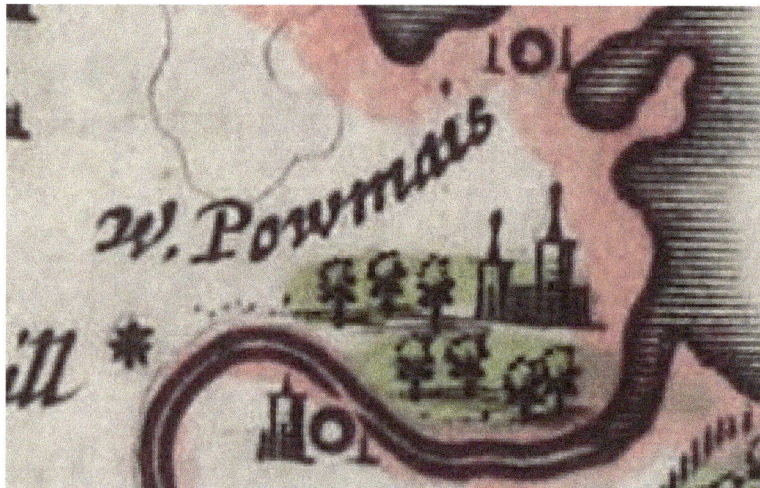

Wester Polmaise as depicted by Blaue where Lady Grange was imprisoned, reproduced with the permission of the National Library of Scotland.

sides. The estate seems to have first been built in the 1400s, and it's likely that the original Wester Polmaise was a tower house. It was all demolished in the middle of the 20th century, and there is nothing but a lumpy field left (281295, 692190, 56° 06′ 28″ N 3° 54′ 37″ W).

However, there remains a much darker secret associated with the house. It is apparently where Lady Grange was held against her will for a few months in 1732. But who was Lady Grange? Well, Rachel Chiesley to give her her maiden name, (1679–1745), was the wife of Lord Grange—a Scottish lawyer with Jacobite tendencies. After nine children and nearly 25 years of marriage, the Granges divorced and it was not an amicable arrangement. She produced a series of letters implicating her husband in treasonous plots against the Hanoverian Government in London. Her ex-husband had her kidnapped from Edinburgh, and en route to the west she was held in captivity here for a while. She was bundled around the country in secret for years, including places like the Monarch Isles, Skye and St Kilda. She died after being held against her will for 13 years, just as Bonnie Prince Charlie kicked off the '45.

After Steuarthall, the Bannock Burn becomes tidal and is encased in two massive levees, bound tight, protecting the farm land around it, and the view is so large and broad... incredible. We watched three panicked deer jump, bound and hide in stages all along the top of it, all the way to the Forth. The path was a bit tricky; we could either weave our way along the top of the levee amongst

The view across the carse.

The confluence of the Bannock Burn and the Forth... and a lot of mud!

the alder saplings or trudge through the mud in the fields—and, of course, there are no end of barbed wire fences. We went at low tide, so we got a great view of rippling tidal mud all the way down; endless repetition and variation, almost fractal.

The Forth: One River with Many Names and Functions

Eventually we hit the confluence. It was a cold, windy November, but we hunkered down out of the wind and took in the view. No other river in Scotland has been named as many times as the Forth, as far as anyone can tell. It has had at least nine other names, having been called *Bodotria, Sinus Orientalis, Mare Freisicum, Froch, Scots Ford, Gweryd, Scottewattre, Ihwdenemur* and *Myrkvifiord*. In Gaelic, 'Forth' is likely to have derived from '*foir*' or '*fraigh*', which means edge or limit, so perhaps the 'edge' of Scotland? Certainly one medieval author described the Battle of Bannockburn as lying on the boundary between Scotland and Britain. The name got a bit of a harder edge from the invading Vikings 1,000 years ago, who added a 'fjord' element to it. The oldest name, *Bodotria*, was recorded by the invading Romans and is probably close to what to what the Celts at Castlewood Hill dun called it. The name seems to come from Gaelic for silent or deaf... so perhaps the Silent One? Might this be the name of a lost God or Goddess?

From the heights of Dumyat to the north, looming above us, the true beauty and scale

The windings of the Forth from Dumyat and the whisky bonds and the base at Bandeath.

of the Forth and all of its windings are revealed: 24 miles of river squeezed across 4 miles as the crow flies; a massive slippery snake of a river, or as 18th century poet Hector MacNeil put it:

Ah! winding Forth!—smooth wandering tide!
O' Strevlin's[76] peerless plain the pride.

This river was the best ally Wallace and Bruce ever had, a source of wealth for centuries, a trade route, a frontier and a barrier for everyone from the Romans to the Jacobites. In later years it became a centre of industry and defences, and was the base of the British Home Fleet. The Forth was described in 1916 as 'the most powerful naval fortress in the British Empire, and probably therefore, in the world' by General George K Scott-Moncrieff. There is nothing left to see from here, but if you have the time—on another day—visit Bandeath and the massive munitions store, where missiles used in the Falklands War were stored and where we urge you to see the World War I railway-mounted crane before it topples into the Forth.

Throughout the medieval period, the river was also was an enormous source of food. The salmon fishing here was amongst the richest in Europe, and the rights to catch them had been granted by David I to Cambuskenneth Abbey. Now, as we have heard, the economy suffered a catastrophic collapse immediately after the Battle of

The World War I Bandeath crane.

Bannockburn and, naturally, local people turned to the river. As a consequence, there were a series of court cases—in particular, a Royal Mandate of the 27th July 1366 asserts Cambuskenneth's rights and found that certain burgesses of Stirling had violently attacked and broken fishing traps on the Forth. Hungry people do desperate things, and Stirling had been at the core of the Wars of Independence for nearly 40 years by this point, so who can blame them?

Whisky Galore!
Right in front of us on the other side of the Forth is a series of warehouses. What's in them? Why, whisky by the gallon; enough to float a boat, enough to get Scotland drunk (maybe not, but we could always try). In fact this is the largest volume of whisky held under one roof in the world. Apparently the atmosphere is perfect, right next to the river! It may have been our imagination, but we were sure we could smell it—and we felt a drouth coming on.

Here is another burst of local pride: Clackmannanshire is the birthplace of the world whisky industry. A multi-billion pound industry, and it all began just a few minutes upstream from this spot. Kennetpans was the largest distillery in Scotland by the 1730s and was run by the Stein family, and included the first Boulton & Watt steam engine in Scotland. The Haigs then married into the Stein family and kicked off a massive brand still going today—and yes, General Haig was a family member. If that wasn't enough, the Steins went on to found Jameson's in Dublin (so sorry, my Irish cousins, Jameson's Whiskey should really be spelt 'whisky'). Anyway, the distillery was shut down in the 1820s and the ruins are still visible from the road or the river, and the

The confluence, the swan and the bond!

owners are trying to restore them—a very worthy project.

The End

Still, the walk was over. As we trudged back, a solitary swan followed us home up the burn, pushing against the current, beautifully oblivious to the wars, the deaths, the lives, the poems and the songs of this muddy trickle! We hope you'll agree with us that our wee jaunt from Nova Scotia, through the fish farms, the Romans and Celts, through the Battle of Bannockburn, the witches, poets, tartan and whisky demonstrates that we were right to call the Bannock Burn the most famous burn in the world.

We hope you enjoyed the book, and that you do the walk yourself. Remember the Right to Roam—you are allowed to be here. Don't let anyone deter you, but please respect the land you walk across and the people whose livelihoods depend on it.

* * *

Endnotes

66) This is of course is the opening stanza of 'Such a Parcel of Rogues in a Nation', Burns' response to the Union of the Scottish and English Parliaments in 1707.

67) We are absolutely certain that just like Woodstock or The Beatles playing the Cavern, far more people would claim to be with Bruce than were ever

actually there! Failure is an orphan but success has many parents.

68) Probably quilted jackets stuffed with cotton.

69) Murray is briefly in this, but blink and you will miss him. Filmed over two years and two excavations, his TV debut lies mostly on the cutting room floor.

70) According to research conducted by the late Alasdair Ross and presented at a conference in Stirling in November 2019 by his colleague Michael Penman. To add insult to injury, this also marked the start of a climate decline and average temperatures dropped leading to even more famine.

71) If you stay on this you will after 10 minutes come across one of the few remaining cantilever railway bridges left in Scotland – based, so they say, on a design by our pal Thomas Telford.

72) A small book by Archie Bone 'Polmaise 3 and 4 Mining Fatalities' records the fatal accidents of 55 miners between 1906 and 1965 who worked under our feet; the youngest, John Moore, was 15 and the oldest, Alexander Rennie, was 71.

73) Please feel free to think of the businessman/politician/sportsman/quisling of your choice.

74) We thought about buying this map... but as both us are tight we didn't, it's available free online at the National Map Library of Scotland!

75) The Stewart name was originally the hereditary position of Steward to the Royal Household, which was re-spelt Stuart after Mary Queen of Scots went to France.

76) Stirling.

THANKS AND ACKNOWLEDGEMENTS

Therese McCormick edited the text and drew the maps.

Andrea Cook picked Ian and Murray up on a couple of very wet cold days!

Thanks to the staff at Eaglesham Parish Church and Carswell Centre who guided us round the Gemmell statues. Thank you to Mr William Gillies for the information on the lava battle axe and for kindly supplying the image of the aforementioned artefact. Thanks also to Michael Carvell, who owns the North Third Pump House and gave Ian a tour.

Thanks to Alasdair Tollemache, who gave us a tour of his house and the many coat hooks. Campbell Chesterman and Alan Leishman who supplied Ian with full access to their archive and information of the crash excavation site of the spitfire 'Gibraltar', and its full flight history. To James Ignacio, who provided images of the spitfire and information of the fundraising carried out by the people of Gibraltar that enable the spitfire to be built. To Gerard Van Coelenberge of Belgian Senior Aviators Association, who made contact on our behalf with the pilot's family and provided the pilot's history, and to Renaud Flamant, Belgian Defence Attache who made this possible. Janet Crowe, who let Ian handle the remainder of Betty's yarn that made the socks for the Tsar. Professor Jim Hardie, who identified the rare, long-winged, water Cricket, *Velia Caprai*. Stuart Malcolm, who gave Ian a tour of the Milton Flour Mill. Donald MacDonald provided an image of the racing at Corbie Wood. Margaret Meiklewood provided an account and several images of her connections to Corbie Wood. Bob Dougal kindly supplied the image of

Sonny Boy winning Race 1 at Corbie Wood on 21st October 2007.

Not forgetting the local knowledge of Bannockburn, its mills and its characters freely revealed to Ian by Stuart Campbell, Robert Aitken, John White, Dennis Canavan and Bennie Tortolano, the latter providing the Italian connection. Gordon Allan for his insight into the world of Sulky racing, and Richard Grierson, our liaison with Scottish Water. A huge thank you from Ian to his friend and amateur historian Allan Meek, who provided invaluable support and encouragement.

George Haggerty provided an image of a Hawkie pottery model. Elena Obuhovich of the State Hermitage Museum, St. Petersburg, Russia, helped us get a copy of the portrait of Tsar Alexander I. The Blaue map was reproduced under a Commons Licence with the permission of the National Library of Scotland. The image of Mousa broch is reproduced under a Creative Commons licence from Geograph UK (6736672) and was taken by Sandy Gerrard, and was licensed under the Creative Commons Attribution-Share Alike 2.0 Generic license (*https://creativecommons.org/licenses/by-sa/2.0/deed.en*). The Jim Bowie monument in New Boston, Bowie County was taken and provided by Paul Ridenour. William Muirhead provided a picture of Beaton's Mill on fire. Mr Dufton provided a photograph of the mineral railway.

Thanks also to Charles Allan Ingles, Jim Steven and Derek Mason who provided some excellent images of Corbiewood, but which unfortunately we didn't use.

ABOUT THE AUTHORS

Dr Murray Cook is Stirling Council's Archaeologist and is from Leith originally, though he also lived and went to school in Edinburgh. He lives in Stirling with a long-suffering wife, three teenage girls and two pesky but loveable cats. He has undertaken numerous excavations across the region and published over 40 books and articles. He won a Stirling's Provost Award in 2018 for his work for the Council, where he has helped raise over £300,000 to be spent on community archaeology and research and has even got invited to see the Queen at Holyrood Palace, along with a few hundred others! He has appeared on several TV programmes, and has sometime even been paid! He writes a regular column in the *Stirling Observer* and runs Stirling Archaeology, a Facebook page dedicated to Stirling's fantastic heritage!:

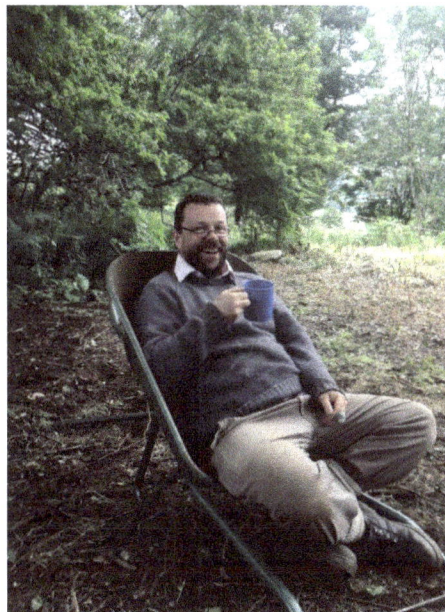

Murray pictured hard at work on location at a dig site!
Photo by Sue Mackay.

https://www.facebook.com/Stirling-Archaeology-176144165815143/

Murray studied at Edinburgh University worked first for AOC Archaeology, rising from subcontractor to Commercial Director. His PhD, which has a rather long and boring title, was based on 10 years of research in Aberdeenshire on settlement patterns between 2000 BC and AD 1000:

https://www.scottishheritagehub.com/content/case-study-kintore-aberdeenshire-shining-light-black-hole/

He is an Honorary Research Fellow at Stirling University, a Fellow of the Society of Antiquaries of Scotland, runs an occasional course at Forth Valley College on Stirling and likes to do it in ditches (archaeology, that is!). He also co-runs regular training digs open to all under the name Rampart Scotland:

http://www.rampartscotland.co.uk/

A series of recorded lectures by Murray on Stirling's history are available at the Bannockburn House YouTube Channel:

http://www.youtube.com/channel/UC4z6NLizcLmtxpSZ9zphoBg/videos/

Archaeology is at first glance an off-putting word, easy to say but hard to spell and Murray has been called the Council's Archivist and Architect before. But he believes that archaeology should be open to all, it is our shared past and it belong to everyone, so barriers should be removed. On this basis Murray runs a series of free walks, lectures and digs through the year to allow people to explore their past, and is open to everyone.

Ian McNeish was born in 1946, in Falkirk. That not only made him a Bairn, but also a Bulge Baby. His formative years in the post-War period were spent in Bonnybridge then Balloch. His early employment was with Carron Ironworks in Falkirk and then Ferranti Limited in Edinburgh, before heading south for a time to Cosser Electronics where he worked as an Organisation and Methods Officer in the electronic manufacturing sector. He then came back home to a job with Aberdeen-shire County Council where, in addition to examining work methods and producing detailed project management reports, he also liaised with staff, unions and management.

In 1974 Ian joined Ross and Sutherland Constabulary, and in seven months was trusted to police in a single station officer role within a rural area of Scotland with a population of six thousand people. In 1978 Ian transferred to Central Scotland Police where he rose to the rank of Chief Inspector, before retiring in 2004.

In the police service Ian gained a Higher National Certificate in police studies, as well as a certificate on Strategic Investigation and a certificate on Structured Debriefing. He is a trained Emergencies Planning officer and successfully completed his Strategic Chief Inspector's course at the Scottish Police College. He trained at the Home Office Crime Prevention Centre, and gained certificates in Crime Prevention and Community Safety as well as Architectural Liaison and Designing Out Crime.

In 1992 Ian was seconded to work within the Policy Unit of Central Regional Council to develop a strategy on community safety, the first officer to take on that role within a Regional Council in

Scotland. The strategy, entitled 'Switched on to Safety', was successful and recognised by the Secretary of State for Scotland's Advisory Group on Sustainable Development. It was highlighted in the white paper 'This Common Inheritance, 1996'. The strategy was further recognised by the UK National Council for the United Nations Conference on Human Settlements as one of the top Best Practice examples in the UK and presented at the Habitat ll United Nations City Summit Conference in Istanbul in June 1996.

On returning to the force, Ian continued his career in Falkirk and then as Local Unit Commander based in Bo'ness. He was promoted to Officer in Charge of Community Safety at Police Headquarters, and took charge of the force's Safety in Communities strategy with particular responsibility for Youth Crime, Safety in Communities, Diversity, Drug Education and liaison with partner agencies, Victims of Crime, and general Crime Prevention issues.

In that role, Ian acted as senior police advisor to the Scottish Office Environment Department when they put together and published their Planning Advice Note 46, entitled 'Planning For Crime Prevention'. He was also responsible for planning the booklet on women's safety entitled *Talking Sense/Seeing Sense*, participating in its writing and editing, as well as advising the Scottish Office on production of the video of the same name. 300,000 copies of the booklet were printed, as well as scores of the video, for use throughout Scotland.

On leaving the police service, Ian set up his own company advising small businesses on policy issues as well as carrying out investigations on employment disputes and preparing reports. Ian has also chaired several internal discipline hearings and produced written judgements. He also was Chairman of the board of Signpost Recovery, and for about eighteen months managed the project.

As a consequence of the foregoing he has amassed a wealth of experience carrying out investigations and producing reports for the criminal justice system and the internal police discipline system, as well as strategic reports and latterly reports and judgements of disputes in the employment arena.

Ian has also carried out several in-depth investigations involving employment disputes and reported his findings to an employment lawyer.

His spare time is taken up with mountaineering, for a time being in Mountain Rescue. He has found time to ascend Mont Blanc and climb all the Munros. He also cycles and has some long distance treks to his name, including cycling from Edinburgh to Paris. He plays competitive curling and also coaches beginners. He did play golf, but cut back on that as he could not spare the time. He has a family: three boys and six grandchildren. When he is not employed with any or all of the above, he writes.

Digging into Stirling's Past
Uncovering the Secrets of Scotland's Smallest City

By Murray Cook

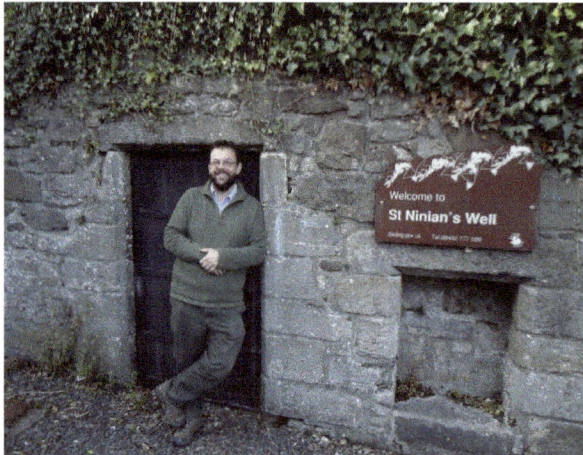

Stirling is Scotland's smallest city and one of its newest. But, strangely, it's also the ancient capital and one of the most important locations in all of Scottish history. If you wanted to invade or to resist invasion, you did it at Stirling. It has witnessed Celts, Romans, Britons, Picts, Scots, Angles, Vikings, Edward I, William Wallace, Robert the Bruce, Edward II, Oliver Cromwell, Bonnie Prince Charlie, the Duke of Cumberland, and even played a decisive role in D-Day.

This huge history has left its mark all over this tiny place. Stirling is Scotland's best preserved medieval city, boasting one of Europe's finest Renaissance palaces, the world's oldest football, Mary Queen of Scots' coronation, James III's grave and murder scene, the site of a successful 16th century assassination of Scotland's head of state, Scotland's first powered and unpowered flights, Scotland's biggest royal rubbish dump, one of Scotland's earliest churches, Scotland's two most important battles, vitrified forts, Scotland's oldest and best preserved Royal Park, connections to King Arthur and the Vikings, Britain's last beheading, Scotland's largest pyramid – and its oldest resident is 4000 years old!

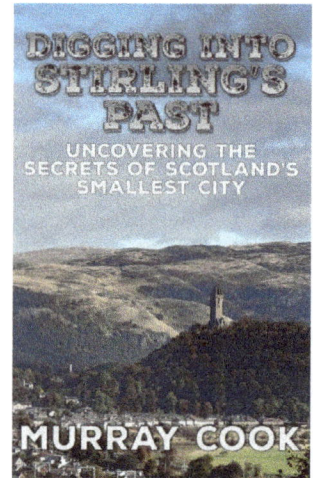

This book tells Stirling's story through its secret nooks and crannies; the spots the tourists overlook and those that the locals have forgotten or never visited. Join Stirling's Burgh Archaeologist, Dr Murray Cook, as he takes you on a tour of a fascinating city's history which is full of heroes and battles, grave robbing, witch trials, bloody beheadings, violent sieges, Jacobite plots, assassins, villains, plagues, Kings and Queens... and much, much more besides.

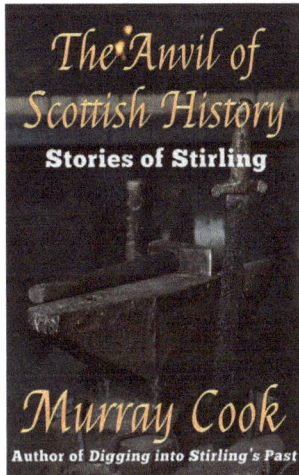

The Anvil of Scottish History
Stories of Stirling

By Murray Cook

Stirling was Scotland's ancient capital, and it remains its best preserved medieval city with its remarkable city walls and late medieval hospital, the oldest royal park, as well as one of the most striking Renaissance palaces in all of Europe. It is home to the world's oldest football and curling stone – and the home of tartan. Stirling was the grounds for the two most important battles in Scottish history as well as having fought Romans, Angles, Picts, Vikings, the English, other Scots, Oliver Cromwell, Jacobites and the Hanoverians, and it even played a key role in the preparations for D-Day. It is the place where our identity and indeed our very existence has been forged and repeatedly tested: the anvil of Scottish history.

This beautiful city sits at the lowest crossing point of the River Forth. This means that every army that ever invaded or resisted invasion had to cross the river at Stirling. So, for the last 2000 years, blood and treasure were lost and heroes and villains created in a perpetual struggle for the control of this key location. This means that almost every single aspect of Scotland's history either impacts, or is impacted by, this amazing place.

Take a fascinating journey through the centuries with Stirling's Burgh Archaeologist, Dr Murray Cook, as he considers the complex and lively history of this unique royal city. From prehistory to the Home Guard, he charts the changing face of Stirling over the course of millennia, detailing some extraordinary archaeological finds and many little-known historical facts. Prepare to discover Stirling's secrets and mysteries for yourself!

Bannockburn and Stirling Bridge
Exploring Scotland's Two Greatest Battles

By Murray Cook

The Scottish Wars of Independence: a titanic struggle over the fate of the Scottish nation which made heroes of Robert the Bruce and William Wallace, and saw many clashes that have gone down as among the most significant in the country's history. None, however, were to be quite as momentous as the epic Battles of Stirling Bridge and Bannockburn.

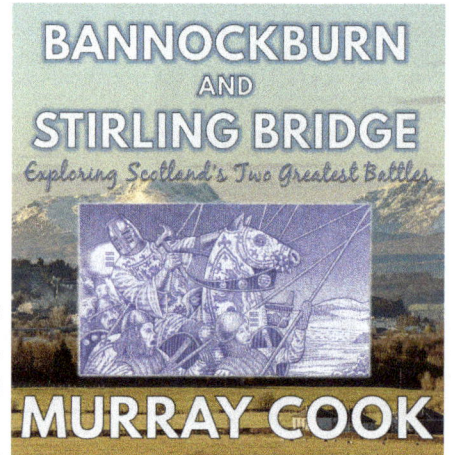

In this book, archaeologist Dr Murray Cook revisits these critical campaigns with reference to his many excavations around the area and the exciting historical discoveries that are still being unearthed to this very day. He explains the background of the battles and the personalities involved, describes the action that took place on those fateful days, and discusses the far-reaching impact the Wars of Independence had on the future of Scotland.

Bannockburn and Stirling Bridge culminates in a five-stage walk around Stirling and the surrounding area in which the author describes the ways in which the Wars of Independence shaped the city's destiny: an influence which can still be witnessed today through the many different historical sites and archaeological finds located throughout the vicinity. He brings the past alive with detailed illustrations drawn from the tumultuous events of bygone centuries, and encourages his readers to seek out the nation's vibrant history for themselves.

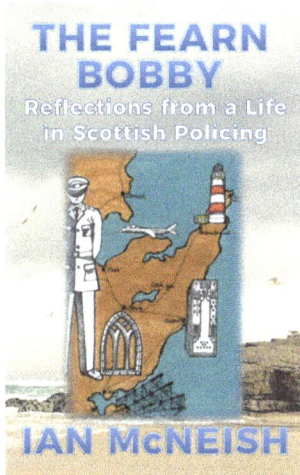

The Fearn Bobby
Reflections from a Life in Scottish Policing

By Ian McNeish

'It's all about the community', the words of Kenneth Ross, Chief Constable of Ross and Sutherland Constabulary, guided Ian McNeish through thirty years of police service. They were true then, back in 1974, and they are true now.

Ian held a police warrant card for three decades, serving communities across Scotland. In that time, his work saw him moving from the northerly constabulary where he policed the rural Hill of Fearn to the social challenges that presented themselves amongst the urban landscape of Central Scotland. From his formative years in post-War Scotland through to his application to join the police service, Ian has led a rich and varied professional life that ranged from working in iron foundries to building electronic parts for the Kestrel Jump Jet and legendary Concorde aircraft. But once he had joined the police service, he found himself faced with a whole new range of life-changing experiences – some of them surprising, a few even shocking, but all of them memorable.

Leading the reader through his involvement in front line situations, Ian explains the effects of anti-social behaviour and attending criminal court appearances, in addition to dealing with death and the responsibilities of informing those left behind. He considers topics such as ethics, public interest, police and firearms, drug issues, causes of crime, and a lot more besides.

In a career where his duties ranged from policing national strikes to providing comfort and support through personal tragedies, Ian advanced through the ranks and saw first-hand the vital importance of effective management and good teamwork. Whether as the 'Fearn Bobby', policing a remote countryside outpost, as a seconded officer working for the Chief Executive of a Regional Council, or as a Local Unit Commander in Bo'ness, Ian always knew the importance of putting the community first. Comparing today's policing techniques with his own professional experiences and examining both the good times and the harrowing pitfalls of the job, his account of life in the force is heartfelt, entertaining, and always completely honest.

From Dumyat to Mont Blanc
Being Alive with Mountains

By Ian McNeish

Born in the Central Scotland town of Bonnybridge, Ian McNeish may have seemed an unlikely climbing enthusiast. The closest 'peak' to his home was Cowden Hill, which at an elevation of 55.4 metres is only the 14,650th highest in Britain! But from these early experiences on the hills, encouragement from friends and colleagues soon saw Ian embarking on a lifelong adventure which would see him climbing Munros and Corbetts alike.

Whether cycling through the Outer Hebrides for charity or white-water rafting in New Zealand, Ian is someone who has seen life. But nothing could have prepared him for facing the biggest climbing challenge of his career when he tackled the famous peak of Mont Blanc—the highest mountain in the Alps, with a summit 4,808 metres above sea level.

From his experiences in Mountain Rescue Teams to not one but two successful attempts at Scotland's famous cross-country Ultimate Challenge, join Ian as he relates amazing stories of some of the most stunning places in the world. He will reveal what it means to truly be alive in the mountains.

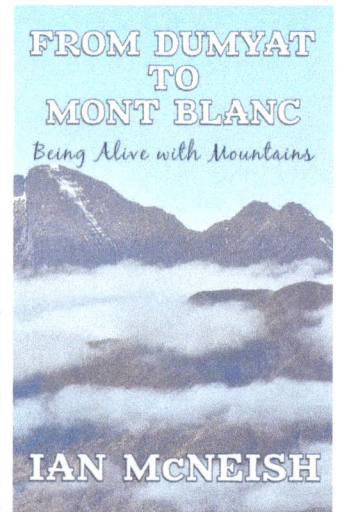

For details of new and forthcoming books from Extremis Publishing, including our monthly podcasts, please visit our official website at:

www.extremispublishing.com

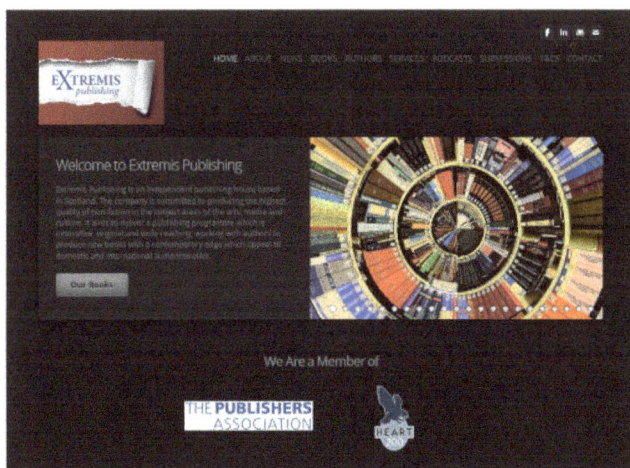

or follow us on social media at:

www.facebook.com/extremispublishing

www.linkedin.com/company/extremis-publishing-ltd-/

Milton Keynes UK
Ingram Content Group UK Ltd.
UKHW050047310823
427785UK00004BA/24

9 781739 854331